INTRODUCTION ...

A few points about this revision guide ...

- It is matched perfectly to the new specification from AQA:

SCIENCE: DOUBLE AWARD COORDINATED - Specification B

So it contains everything the pupil needs to know, ...

        ... and nothing more.

- The 'Contents' pages are cross-referenced to the specification reference.

- Each section is condensed into a single 'Key Points' page. This enables a quick final recap prior to examination and also builds pupils' confidence in that they can see their task before them on a single page.

- Each section concludes with a set of summary questions. These are, of necessity, brief but can be supplemented by our brilliant volume of 'pupil worksheets' which are written page for page to this guide (see inside back cover).

- Slang words and colloquialisms are avoided in favour of plain, good old-fashioned English.

- The new layout, with improved diagrams, provides a more spacious, user-friendly feel.

- The layout has been changed slightly in order to reflect the specification more sympathetically and to provide six approximately equal sections.

- The reduction in the amount of 'Higher' material in the new specification means that it makes more sense than ever before to combine both 'Higher' and 'Foundation' material in the one guide. This, of course, allows much greater flexibility in switching between tiers.

> ╱╱╱╱╱╱╱╱╱╱╱╱╱╱╱╱╱╱╱╱╱╱╱╱ **HIGHER TIER** ╱╱
> **All the 'Higher' material is clearly indicated by RED boxes.**

Mary James

Mary James – **Editor**

● CONTENTS

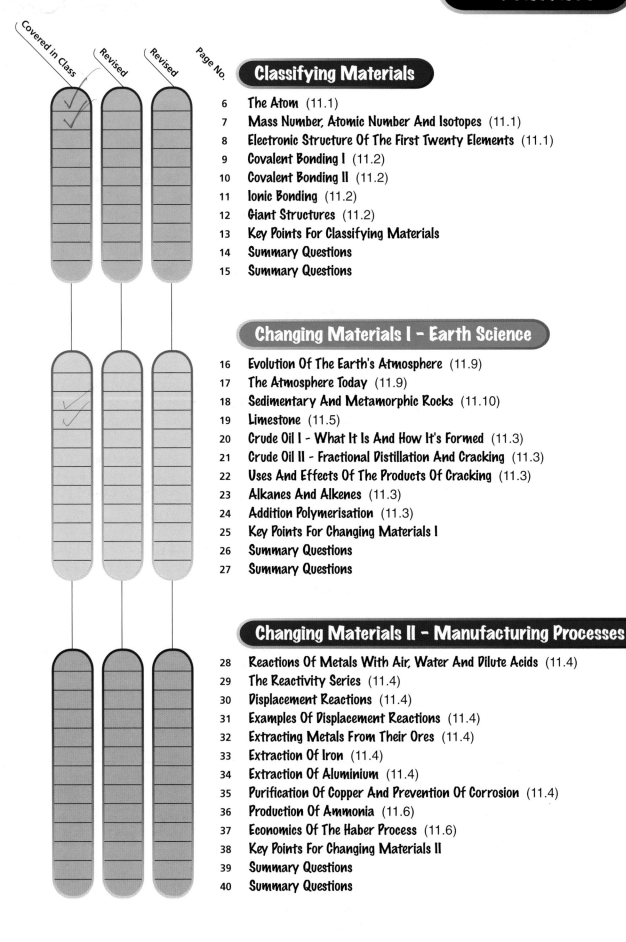

Covered In Class
Revised
Revised
Page No.

• CONTENTS

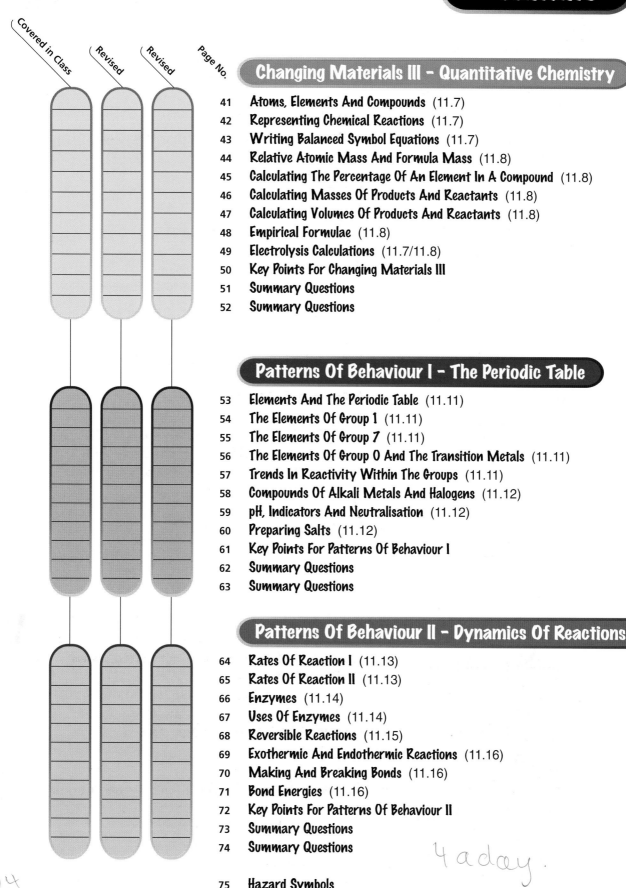

Covered in Class

Revised

Revised

Page No.

4 a day.

24/7

24

*Numbers in brackets refer to Specification reference numbers

HOW TO USE THIS REVISION GUIDE

- Don't just sit back and read this guide. Learn actively by constantly testing yourself without looking at the text.

- When you have revised a small sub-section or a diagram, PLACE A BOLD TICK AGAINST IT, and also tick the 'Covered In Class' and 'Revised' sections of the contents pages as you progress.
  This is great for your self-confidence.

- Jot down anything which will help you to remember – no matter how trivial it may seem.

- Use the actual pages within a section for your revision and link them to the information in the 'Key Points' pages. Only use the 'Key Points' pages on their own for a last minute recap before your examination.

---- HIGHER TIER ----

ONLY PUPILS DOING HIGHER TIER SHOULD REVISE THE MATERIAL IN THE RED BOXES.

SOME IMPORTANT FACTS ABOUT YOUR EXAMINATION

- You will have THREE PAPERS lasting 1 HOUR 30 MINUTES EACH.

- Each paper will consist of 90 marks and represent $26^{2}/_{3}$ % of the total marks available.

- All papers will consist of compulsory structured questions of different lengths, incorporating calculations and data-response, and will provide opportunities for answers written in continuous prose.
  The marking of these will take into account the quality of written communication.

- Candidates may use a calculator for all three papers.

  PAPER 1: LIFE PROCESSES AND LIVING THINGS
  PAPER 2: MATERIALS AND THEIR PROPERTIES
  PAPER 3: PHYSICAL PROCESSES

NOTES

THE ATOM

John Dalton

The idea that everything is made up of very small particles is not new! The ancient Greeks were the first to propose such ideas 2500 years ago. Unfortunately they were unable to provide evidence for their ideas and so it was rejected until 1808, when a school teacher, John Dalton, carried out some experiments and re-introduced the idea of these very small particles which he called ATOMS. His theory stated that the atoms of a particular element are all the same, while different elements are made up of different atoms.

Structure Of The Atom

Today we know that all substances are made of atoms. There are about 100 different kinds of atom and each one is made up of even smaller particles ...
The central nucleus is made up of PROTONS and NEUTRONS (with one exception) and is surrounded by ELECTRONS arranged in ENERGY LEVELS (or shells).

This is an atom of fluorine:

The nucleus is surrounded by orbiting electrons ✗ which are negatively charged and arranged in shells. A fluorine atom contains 9 electrons.

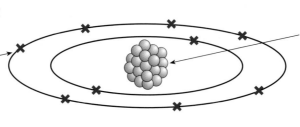

This is the nucleus. It contains protons ◯ which are positively charged and neutrons ◯ which are neutral.
The nucleus is small and heavy. A fluorine atom contains 9 protons and 10 neutrons.

ATOMIC PARTICLE		RELATIVE MASS	RELATIVE CHARGE
PROTON	◯	1	+1
NEUTRON	◯	1	0
ELECTRON	✗	1/1840 (almost nothing)	-1

- An atom has the same number of protons as electrons, so the atom as a whole has no electrical charge.
- A proton has the same mass as a neutron.
- The mass of an electron is negligible ie. nearly nothing compared to a proton or neutron.
- A substance which contains only one sort of atom is called an element.

Here are three other atoms ...

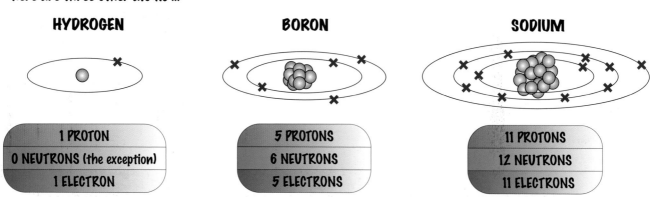

HYDROGEN

| 1 PROTON |
| 0 NEUTRONS (the exception) |
| 1 ELECTRON |

BORON

| 5 PROTONS |
| 6 NEUTRONS |
| 5 ELECTRONS |

SODIUM

| 11 PROTONS |
| 12 NEUTRONS |
| 11 ELECTRONS |

Mass Number And Atomic Number

Atoms of an element can be described very conveniently; take the fluorine atom ...

The **MASS NUMBER** is ...

... the TOTAL NUMBER OF PROTONS AND NEUTRONS IN THE ATOM. → 19

¹⁹₉F

ELEMENT SYMBOL IN THIS CASE, THE ELEMENT FLUORINE

The **ATOMIC NUMBER** (Proton Number) is ...

... the NUMBER OF PROTONS IN THE ATOM. → 9

The ATOMIC NUMBER gives the NUMBER OF PROTONS which is equal to the NUMBER OF ELECTRONS ...
... because atoms have no overall charge.

NUMBER OF NEUTRONS = MASS NUMBER – ATOMIC NUMBER

EXAMPLES

$^{1}_{1}H$ **HYDROGEN**
1 proton
1 electron
0 neutrons (1-1)

$^{4}_{2}He$ **HELIUM**
2 protons
2 electrons
2 neutrons (4-2)

$^{16}_{8}O$ **OXYGEN**
8 protons
8 electrons
8 neutrons (16-8)

$^{23}_{11}Na$ **SODIUM**
11 protons
11 electrons
12 neutrons (23-11)

Isotopes

ALL ATOMS of a particular ELEMENT have the SAME NUMBER OF PROTONS.
Atoms of different elements have different numbers of protons.
However some atoms of the SAME ELEMENT can have DIFFERENT NUMBERS OF NEUTRONS ...
... these are called ISOTOPES.
They are easy to spot because they have the SAME ATOMIC NUMBER but a DIFFERENT MASS NUMBER.

EXAMPLE   CHLORINE ...

$^{35}_{17}Cl$ 17 protons
17 electrons
18 neutrons (35-17)

$^{37}_{17}Cl$ 17 protons
17 electrons
20 neutrons (37-17)

EXAMPLE   CARBON ...

$^{12}_{6}C$ 6 protons
6 electrons
6 neutrons (12-6)

$^{13}_{6}C$ 6 protons
6 electrons
7 neutrons (13-6)

$^{14}_{6}C$ 6 protons
6 electrons
8 neutrons (14-6)

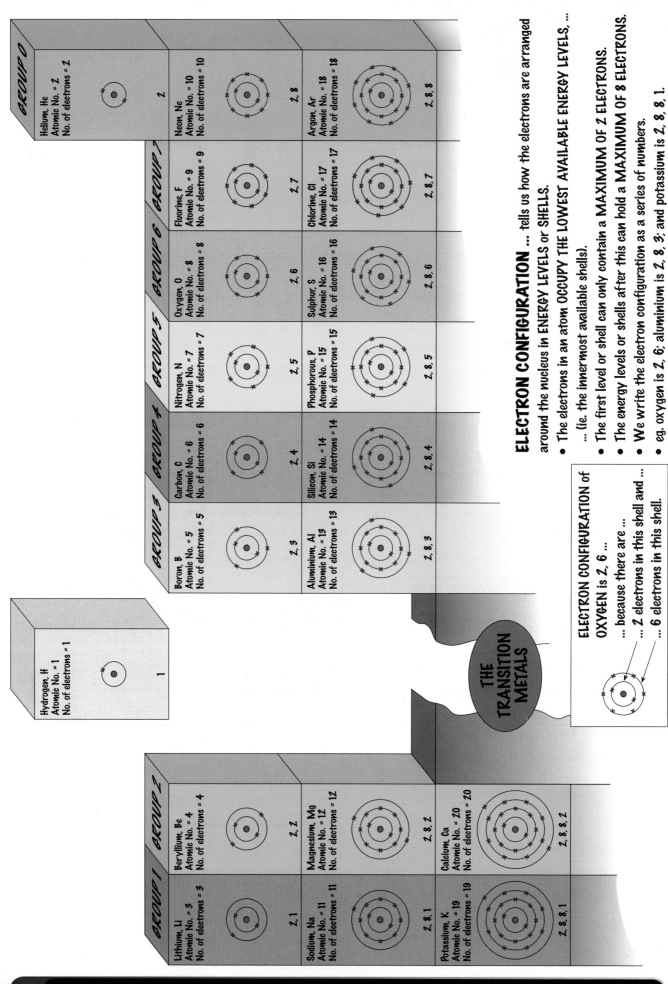

ELECTRON CONFIGURATION ... tells us how the electrons are arranged around the nucleus in ENERGY LEVELS or SHELLS.

- The electrons in an atom OCCUPY THE LOWEST AVAILABLE ENERGY LEVELS, ... (ie. the innermost available shells).
- The first level or shell can only contain a MAXIMUM OF 2 ELECTRONS.
- The energy levels or shells after this can hold a MAXIMUM OF 8 ELECTRONS.
- We write the electron configuration as a series of numbers.
- eg. oxygen is 2, 6; aluminium is 2, 8, 3; and potassium is 2, 8, 8, 1.

ELECTRON CONFIGURATION of OXYGEN is 2, 6 ...
... because there are ...
... 2 electrons in this shell and ...
... 6 electrons in this shell.

THE TRANSITION METALS

GROUP 0

Helium, He
Atomic No. = 2
No. of electrons = 2
2

Neon, Ne
Atomic No. = 10
No. of electrons = 10
2, 8

Argon, Ar
Atomic No. = 18
No. of electrons = 18
2, 8, 8

GROUP 7

Fluorine, F
Atomic No. = 9
No. of electrons = 9
2, 7

Chlorine, Cl
Atomic No. = 17
No. of electrons = 17
2, 8, 7

GROUP 6

Oxygen, O
Atomic No. = 8
No. of electrons = 8
2, 6

Sulphur, S
Atomic No. = 16
No. of electrons = 16
2, 8, 6

GROUP 5

Nitrogen, N
Atomic No. = 7
No. of electrons = 7
2, 5

Phosphorous, P
Atomic No. = 15
No. of electrons = 15
2, 8, 5

GROUP 4

Carbon, C
Atomic No. = 6
No. of electrons = 6
2, 4

Silicon, Si
Atomic No. = 14
No. of electrons = 14
2, 8, 4

GROUP 3

Boron, B
Atomic No. = 5
No. of electrons = 5
2, 3

Aluminium, Al
Atomic No. = 13
No. of electrons = 13
2, 8, 3

Hydrogen, H
Atomic No. = 1
No. of electrons = 1
1

GROUP 1

Lithium, Li
Atomic No. = 3
No. of electrons = 3
2, 1

Sodium, Na
Atomic No. = 11
No. of electrons = 11
2, 8, 1

Potassium, K
Atomic No. = 19
No. of electrons = 19
2, 8, 8, 1

GROUP 2

Beryllium, Be
Atomic No. = 4
No. of electrons = 4
2, 2

Magnesium, Mg
Atomic No. = 12
No. of electrons = 12
2, 8, 2

Calcium, Ca
Atomic No. = 20
No. of electrons = 20
2, 8, 8, 2

- COMPOUNDS are substances in which the atoms of TWO OR MORE ELEMENTS ...
- ... are CHEMICALLY COMBINED (not just mixed together!).

> ATOMS CAN FORM CHEMICAL BONDS BY EITHER ...
> ... (1) SHARING ELECTRONS (COVALENT BONDS), or ...
> ... (2) GAINING OR LOSING ELECTRONS (IONIC BONDS).

- Either way, when atoms form chemical bonds the arrangement of the outermost shell of electrons changes ...
- ... resulting in each atom getting a 'complete' outer shell of electrons.
- For most atoms this is EIGHT ELECTRONS ...
- ... but for the FIVE LIGHTEST ELEMENTS it is only TWO!

The Covalent Bond

This occurs between NON-METAL atoms.
A very strong bond is formed in which ELECTRONS ARE SHARED.
EXAMPLE ... A CHLORINE MOLECULE (made up of two chlorine atoms).

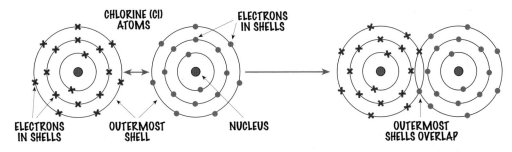

CHLORINE (CI) ATOMS — ELECTRONS IN SHELLS — ELECTRONS IN SHELLS — OUTERMOST SHELL — NUCLEUS — OUTERMOST SHELLS OVERLAP

The atoms BOTH need to gain an electron to fill their outermost energy levels ...

... they achieve this by sharing one pair of electrons in a COVALENT BOND.

> BOTH CHLORINE ATOMS HAVE 8 ELECTRONS IN THEIR OUTERMOST ENERGY LEVEL ...
> ... WHICH MEANS THIS ENERGY LEVEL (SHELL) IS COMPLETE.

Atoms which share electrons often form MOLECULES in which there are ...
... STRONG COVALENT BONDS BETWEEN THE ATOMS IN EACH MOLECULE ...
... but NOT between INDIVIDUAL MOLECULES.

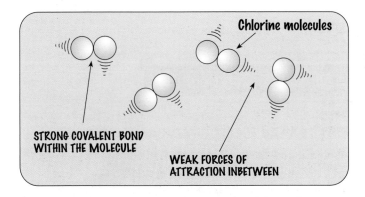

Chlorine molecules

STRONG COVALENT BOND WITHIN THE MOLECULE

WEAK FORCES OF ATTRACTION INBETWEEN

- This means that they usually have LOW MELTING AND BOILING POINTS.

Other Examples

You need to be familiar with the following examples. Also, you need to know three different forms of representing the covalent bonds in each molecule. Two forms are given in the examples below.

1. WATER, H_2O

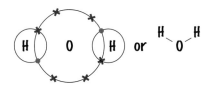

2. AMMONIA, NH_3

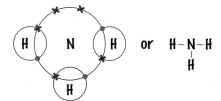

3. HYDROGEN, H_2

4. HYDROGEN CHLORIDE, HCl

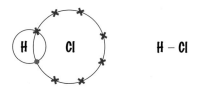

5. METHANE, CH_4

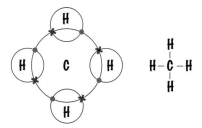

6. OXYGEN, O_2

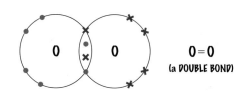

The third form of representing covalent bonds is shown here for an ammonia molecule.

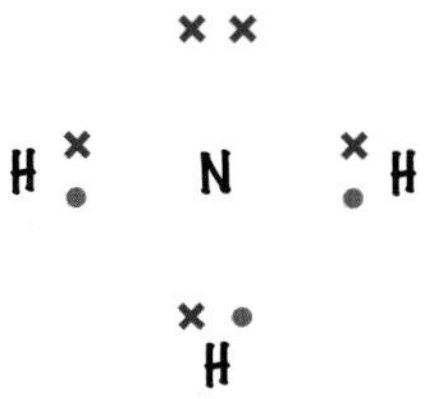

This is perhaps the most confusing method, and unless specifically asked for candidates should stick to the other two methods.

━━ HIGHER TIER ━━

Properties Of Simple Molecular Compounds

These are gases, liquids or solids ...
... which have WEAK INTERMOLECULAR FORCES OF ATTRACTION BETWEEN MOLECULES ...
... unlike the very strong covalent bond that exists between two atoms.
This results in them having LOW MELTING AND BOILING POINTS.
They are also NON-CONDUCTORS of ELECTRICITY ...
... as the molecules do not have an OVERALL ELECTRIC CHARGE.

The Ionic Bond

This occurs between a METAL and a NON-METAL ATOM and involves a TRANSFER OF ELECTRONS ...

... from one atom to the other, to form electrically charged 'atoms' called IONS ...

... each of which has a 'COMPLETE' OUTERMOST ENERGY LEVEL or SHELL.

Atoms which LOSE ELECTRONS become POSITIVELY CHARGED IONS while ...

... atoms which GAIN ELECTRONS become NEGATIVELY CHARGED IONS.

Either way the ions formed have the electronic structure of a noble gas ...

... ie. they have full outermost energy levels.

Ionic compounds are giant structures of ions held together by strong forces of attraction between oppositely charged ions. They have HIGH MELTING and BOILING POINTS.

EXAMPLE 1
Sodium and chlorine ... to form SODIUM CHLORIDE, NaCl

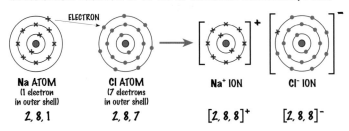

ELECTRON

Na ATOM
(1 electron
in outer shell)
2, 8, 1

Cl ATOM
(7 electrons
in outer shell)
2, 8, 7

Na⁺ ION
$[2, 8, 8]^+$

Cl⁻ ION
$[2, 8, 8]^-$

The SODIUM (Na) ATOM has 1 ELECTRON ...

... in its OUTER SHELL which is TRANSFERRED ...

... to the CHLORINE (Cl) ATOM.

BOTH now have 8 ELECTRONS ...

... in their OUTER SHELL.

The atoms are now IONS ...

... Na^+ and Cl^- ...

... and the COMPOUND FORMED is ...

... SODIUM CHLORIDE, NaCl.

EXAMPLE 2
Calcium and chlorine ... to form CALCIUM CHLORIDE, CaCl₂.

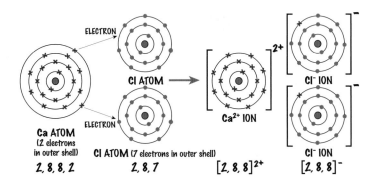

ELECTRON

Cl ATOM

ELECTRON

Ca ATOM
(2 electrons
in outer shell)
2, 8, 8, 2

Cl ATOM (7 electrons in outer shell)
2, 8, 7

Ca²⁺ ION
$[2, 8, 8]^{2+}$

Cl⁻ ION

Cl⁻ ION
$[2, 8, 8]^-$

The CALCIUM (Ca) ATOM has 2 ELECTRONS ...

... in its OUTER SHELL.

A CHLORINE (Cl) ATOM ...

... only 'WANTS' 1 ELECTRON ...

... therefore 2 Cl ATOMS ARE NEEDED.

The atoms are now IONS ...

... Ca^{2+}, Cl^- and Cl^- ...

... and the COMPOUND FORMED is ...

... CALCIUM CHLORIDE, CaCl₂.

EXAMPLE 3
Magnesium and oxygen ... to form MAGNESIUM OXIDE, MgO.

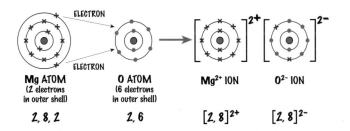

ELECTRON

ELECTRON

Mg ATOM
(2 electrons
in outer shell)
2, 8, 2

O ATOM
(6 electrons
in outer shell)
2, 6

Mg²⁺ ION
$[2, 8]^{2+}$

O²⁻ ION
$[2, 8]^{2-}$

The MAGNESIUM (Mg) ATOM has 2 ELECTRONS ...

... in its OUTER SHELL which are TRANSFERRED ...

... to the OXYGEN (O) ATOM.

BOTH now have 8 ELECTRONS ...

... in their OUTER SHELL.

The atoms are now IONS ...

... Mg^{2+} and O^{2-} ...

... and the COMPOUND FORMED is ...

... MAGNESIUM OXIDE, MgO.

Giant Covalent Structures

Diamond (A Form Of Carbon)

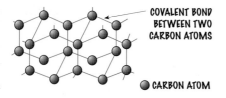

COVALENT BOND BETWEEN TWO CARBON ATOMS

CARBON ATOM

- A GIANT, RIGID COVALENT STRUCTURE (LATTICE) where each carbon atom ...
- ... forms FOUR COVALENT BONDS with other carbon atoms.
- The large number of covalent bonds results in diamond having a <u>VERY HIGH MELTING POINT.</u>

Graphite (A Form Of Carbon)

- A GIANT COVALENT STRUCTURE (LATTICE) in which each carbon atom ...
- ... forms THREE COVALENT BONDS with other carbon atoms ...
- ... in a layered structure in which layers can slide past each other.
- Between layers there are weak forces of attraction ...
- ... resulting in free electrons and so graphite <u>CONDUCTS ELECTRICITY.</u>

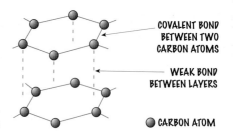

COVALENT BOND BETWEEN TWO CARBON ATOMS

WEAK BOND BETWEEN LAYERS

CARBON ATOM

Silicon Dioxide, SiO_2 (Silica)

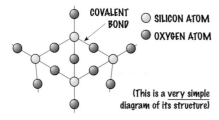

COVALENT BOND

○ SILICON ATOM
● OXYGEN ATOM

(This is a very simple diagram of its structure)

- A GIANT COVALENT STRUCTURE (LATTICE) similar to diamond where each oxygen atom is joined ...
- ... to two silicon atoms and each silicon atom is joined to four oxygen atoms.
- The large number of covalent bonds results in silicon dioxide having a <u>VERY HIGH MELTING POINT.</u>

Giant Ionic Structures

A REGULAR STRUCTURE (GIANT IONIC LATTICE) ...
... held together by the strong forces of attraction ...
... between oppositely charged ions.
This results in them having ...
... HIGH MELTING and BOILING POINTS.
Ionic compounds also CONDUCT ELECTRICITY. ...
... when molten or in solution ...
... because the charged ions are free to move about.

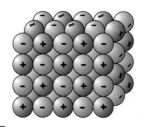

+ POSITIVELY CHARGED IONS

- NEGATIVELY CHARGED IONS

Metals

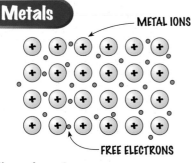

METAL IONS

FREE ELECTRONS

- Metals have a giant structure in which electrons in the highest energy level are free to move through the whole structure. This effectively produces a regular arrangement (lattice) of metal ions in a 'sea of electrons'.

These free electrons ...

- Hold the atoms together in a regular structure.
- Allow the atoms to slide over each other.
- Allow the metal to conduct heat and electricity.

THE ATOM, MASS No., ATOMIC No. AND ISOTOPES

ATOMIC STRUCTURE

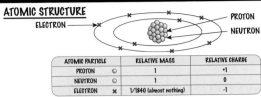

ATOMIC PARTICLE	RELATIVE MASS	RELATIVE CHARGE
PROTON ⊙	1	+1
NEUTRON ○	1	0
ELECTRON ✗	1/1840 (almost nothing)	-1

- An atom has the same number of protons as electrons, so the atom as a whole has no electrical charge.
- A substance which contains only one sort of atom is called an element.

MASS NUMBER AND ATOMIC NUMBER

NUMBER OF NEUTRONS =
MASS NUMBER - ATOMIC NUMBER

MASS NUMBER → 19
ATOMIC NUMBER → 9 **F** ← symbol of the element

ISOTOPES

- All atoms of a particular element have same no. of protons.
- Some atoms of the same element can have different numbers of neutrons - these are called isotopes.

$^{35}_{17}$**Cl** — 17 protons, 17 electrons, 18 neutrons (35-17)

$^{37}_{17}$**Cl** — 17 protons, 17 electrons, 20 neutrons (37-17)

ELECTRON CONFIGURATION

The first shell can hold a maximum of 2 electrons, with each subsequent shell holding a maximum of 8.

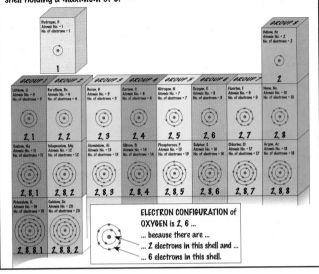

ELECTRON CONFIGURATION of OXYGEN is 2, 6 ...
... because there are ...
... 2 electrons in this shell and ...
... 6 electrons in this shell.

COVALENT BONDING I

THE COVALENT BOND

- Occurs between NON-METAL atoms.
- A very strong bond is formed in which ELECTRONS ARE SHARED resulting in each atom getting a 'complete' outer shell of electrons.

EXAMPLE ...

A CHLORINE MOLECULE (made up of two chlorine atoms).

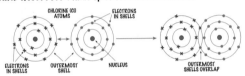

BOTH CHLORINE ATOMS HAVE 8 ELECTRONS IN THEIR OUTERMOST ENERGY LEVEL ...
... WHICH MEANS THIS ENERGY LEVEL (SHELL) IS COMPLETE.

- ATOMS which share electrons often form MOLECULES in which there are STRONG COVALENT BONDS between THE ATOMS IN EACH MOLECULE, but NOT between INDIVIDUAL MOLECULES. This means that they usually have LOW MELTING AND BOILING POINTS.

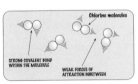

Chlorine molecules

STRONG COVALENT BOND WITHIN THE MOLECULE

WEAK FORCES OF ATTRACTION INBETWEEN

COVALENT BONDING II

SIX EXAMPLES

1. WATER, H_2O

 or H – O – H

2. AMMONIA, NH_3

or H – N – H with H below

3. HYDROGEN, H_2

 H – H

4. HYDROGEN CHLORIDE, HCl

 H – Cl

5. METHANE, CH_4

H – C – H (with H above and below)

6. OXYGEN, O_2

O=O (a DOUBLE BOND)

PROPERTIES OF SIMPLE MOLECULAR COMPOUNDS

These are gases, liquids or solids which have WEAK INTERMOLECULAR FORCES OF ATTRACTION BETWEEN MOLECULES unlike the very strong covalent bond that exists between two atoms.
This results in them having LOW MELTING AND BOILING POINTS.
They are also NON-CONDUCTORS of ELECTRICITY as the molecules do not have an OVERALL ELECTRIC CHARGE.

IONIC BONDING

THE IONIC BOND

- Occurs between a METAL and a NON-METAL atom.
- It involves a TRANSFER OF ELECTRONS from one atom to the other to form electrically charged 'atoms' called IONS ...
  ... each of which has a complete outermost energy level or shell.
- Atoms which lose electrons become positively charged ions and vice versa.

EXAMPLES ...

1. Sodium and chlorine ...
   to form sodium chloride, NaCl

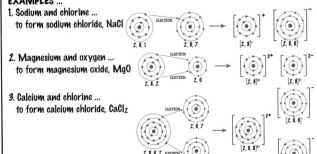

2. Magnesium and oxygen ...
   to form magnesium oxide, MgO

3. Calcium and chlorine ...
   to form calcium chloride, $CaCl_2$

- Ionic compounds are giant structures of ions held together by strong forces of attraction between oppositely charged ions.
- They have HIGH MELTING AND BOILING POINTS

GIANT STRUCTURES

COVALENT STRUCTURES

1. DIAMOND

- Each carbon atom forms 4 covalent bonds with other carbon atoms.
- Very high melting point.

2. GRAPHITE

- Each carbon atom forms 3 covalent bonds in a layered structure in which layers can slide past each other.
- Between layers there are weak forces of attraction resulting in free electrons and so graphite conducts electricity.

3. SILICON DIOXIDE

- Each oxygen atom is joined to 2 silicon atoms and each silicon atom is joined to 4 oxygen atoms.
- Very high melting point.

(This is a very simple diagram of its structure)

IONIC STRUCTURES

- Regular structures with strong forces of attraction between adjacent ions.
- This results in them having HIGH MELTING and BOILING POINTS.
- Conduct electricity when molten or dissolved in water.

METALS

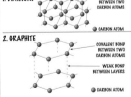

METAL IONS

FREE ELECTRONS

- Structure is a regular arrangement of metal ions in a 'sea of electrons'. These free electrons ...
- ... hold the atoms together in a regular structure.
- ... allow the atoms to slide over each other.
- ... allow the metal to conduct heat and electricity.

1. Fill in the spaces below using the following words (use each one only once)
ELECTRONS, CENTRAL NUCLEUS, ELEMENT, NEUTRONS, ATOM, PROTONS, SHELLS.
All substances are made from atoms. A substance which contains only one sort of _atom_
is called an _element_. The atom consists of a small _central nucleus_ made up of
protons and _neutrons_ surrounded by _electrons_ arranged
in _shells_.

2. Complete the following table.

ATOMIC PARTICLE	RELATIVE MASS	RELATIVE CHARGE
neutron	1-	0
ELECTRON	negligible	1-
Proton	1	1+

3. Why does an atom as a whole have no electrical charge?

4. a) What is mass number? protons + neutrons
   b) What is atomic number? protons / electrons

5. Complete the following table.

ELEMENT	Lithium	Boron	Oxygen	Fluorine	Sodium	Aluminium	Sulphur	iron 26
SYMBOL	$^{7}_{3}Li$	$^{11}_{5}B$	$^{16}_{8}O$	$^{19}_{9}F$	$^{23}_{11}Na$	$^{27}_{13}Al$	$^{32}_{16}S$	$^{56}_{26}Fe$
No. of protons	3	5	8	9	11	13	16	26
No. of neutrons	4	6	8	10	12	14	16	30
No. of electrons	3	5	8	9	11	13	16	26

6. a) What are isotopes? Same no. of electrons (protons) - different neutrons
   b) Here are three isotopes for oxygen. $^{16}_{8}O$ $^{17}_{8}O$ $^{18}_{8}O$
      Which isotope (i) contains 9 neutrons? (ii) is the heaviest? (iii) contains 8 protons?
      2   3   1,2,3

7. Draw diagrams to show the electron configurations for the following atoms a) carbon b) aluminium
   c) chlorine and d) potassium.
   2.4,   2.8.3   2.8.7,   2.8.8.1

8. For the following electron configurations name each element.
   a) 2,3   b) 2,8,4   c) 2,8,8,2.   Boron, Silicon, Calcium

9. Complete the following. The first one has been done for you.

Beryllium, Be	Boron, B	Phosphorus, P	Magnesium, Mg
Atomic No. = 4	Atomic No. = 5	Atomic No. = 15	Atomic No. = 12
No. of Electrons = 4	No. of Electrons = 5	No. of Electrons = 15	No. of Electrons = 12
Electron config. = 2,2.	Electron config. = 2,3	Electron config. = 2,8,5	Electron config. = 2,8,2
Electron config. diagram	Electron config. diagram	Electron config. diagram	Electron config. diagram

10. a) What is the difference between a covalent and an ionic bond? *C – non+non , ion – non+melal*
    b) Draw diagrams to show how
       i)   a hydrogen molecule is made from two hydrogen atoms
       ii) an oxygen molecule is made from two oxygen atoms.
       iii) an ammonia molecule is made from one nitrogen atom and
            three hydrogen atoms.
       iv) a methane molecule is made from one carbon atom and four hydrogen atoms.

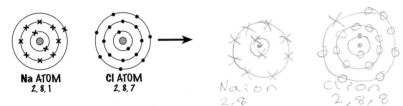

11. a) Why do simple covalent compounds have low melting and boiling points?
    b) Why are simple covalent compounds non-conductors of electricity? *includes no transfer of electron*

12. a) The diagram below shows an incomplete diagram of the ionic bond which occurs between a sodium atom
       and a chlorine atom. Copy and complete the diagram.

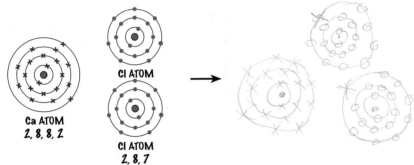

Na ATOM
2, 8, 1

Cl ATOM
2, 8, 7

Na ion
2, 8

Cl ion
2, 8, 8

    b) The diagram below shows an incomplete diagram of the ionic bonds which occur between a calcium atom
       and two chlorine atoms. Copy and complete the diagram.

Ca ATOM
2, 8, 8, 2

Cl ATOM
2, 8, 7

13. Below is a simple diagram showing the structure of diamond and graphite.

COVALENT BOND
BETWEEN TWO
CARBON ATOMS

● CARBON ATOM

COVALENT BOND
BETWEEN TWO
CARBON ATOMS

WEAK BOND
BETWEEN LAYERS

● CARBON ATOM

Explain ....
    a) the difference between the structure of diamond and graphite. *6atoms, 5atoms*
    b) why diamond has a very high melting point.
    c) why graphite conducts electricity.

14. Below is a simple diagram showing the structure of an ionic compound.
    Explain why ...

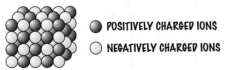

● POSITIVELY CHARGED IONS
○ NEGATIVELY CHARGED IONS

    a) ionic compounds have high melting and boiling points b) ionic compounds conduct electricity.

15. Explain why metals are good conductors of heat and electricity.

Since the formation of the Earth 4.6 billion years ago the atmosphere has changed very dramatically. The timescale, however, is enormous because one billion years is one thousand million years! (1,000,000,000)

COMPOSITION OF THE ATMOSPHERE

TIME SCALE

KEY FACTORS AND EVENTS WHICH SHAPED THE ATMOSPHERE

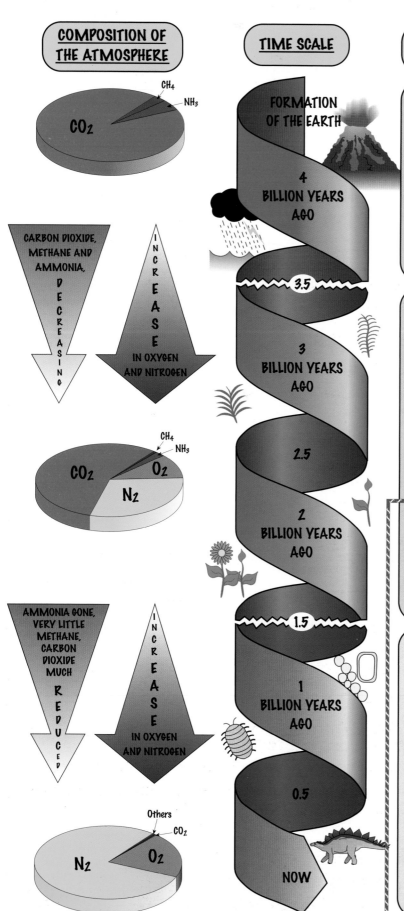

FORMATION OF THE EARTH

Volcanic activity releases ...
- ... mainly CARBON DIOXIDE, and ...
- ... small amounts of METHANE ... ... and AMMONIA.
- WATER VAPOUR is also released which condenses to form the oceans.

4 BILLION YEARS AGO

3.5

Green plants evolve and ...
- CARBON DIOXIDE is reduced as the plants take it in and give out OXYGEN.
- Microorganisms which can't tolerate OXYGEN are killed off.
- Carbon from CARBON DIOXIDE in the air becomes locked up in sedimentary rocks as carbonates and fossil fuels.
- METHANE and AMMONIA react with the OXYGEN now available.

3 BILLION YEARS AGO

2.5

HIGHER TIER

2 BILLION YEARS AGO

- This releases NITROGEN (from the AMMONIA), which is also produced as a result of the action of DENITRIFYING BACTERIA on nitrates from decaying plant material.

1.5

1 BILLION YEARS AGO

- The OXYGEN in the atmosphere is now much increased and some of it is converted into OZONE.
- This OZONE forms a thin layer in the atmosphere which filters out harmful U.V. light from the sun.
- The reduction in harmful ultra-violet light falling onto the surface of the planet allows the evolution of new living organisms.

0.5

NOW

Composition Of The Atmosphere

Our atmosphere has been more or less the same for 200 million years!!!

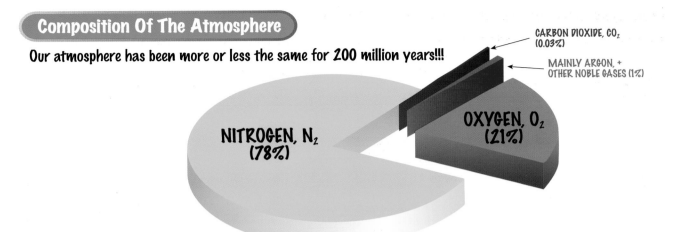

CARBON DIOXIDE, CO_2 (0.03%)

MAINLY ARGON, + OTHER NOBLE GASES (1%)

OXYGEN, O_2 (21%)

NITROGEN, N_2 (78%)

- WATER VAPOUR may also be present in varying quantities (0-3%).

HIGHER TIER

Modern Day Changes To The Level Of Carbon Dioxide In The Atmosphere

The level of CARBON DIOXIDE in the atmosphere is INCREASED due to ...

VOLCANIC ACTIVITY

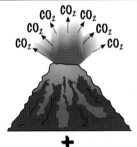

Geological activity moves ...
... CARBONATE ROCKS deep ...
... into the EARTH.

During volcanic activity, ...
... they may release CARBON DIOXIDE ...
... back into the atmosphere.

+

BURNING OF FOSSIL FUELS

The burning of the carbon, ...
... which has been locked up ...
... in FOSSIL FUELS for ....

... millions of years, releases ...
... CARBON DIOXIDE into ...
... the atmosphere.

The level of CARBON DIOXIDE in the atmosphere is REDUCED by...

THE REACTION BETWEEN CARBON DIOXIDE AND SEA WATER

- Increased CARBON DIOXIDE in the atmosphere increases the reaction between ...

... CARBON DIOXIDE and SEA WATER, which produces INSOLUBLE CARBONATES (mainly calcium) ...

... which are deposited as SEDIMENT and SOLUBLE HYDROGENCARBONATES (mainly calcium and magnesium).

Unfortunately this reaction does NOT remove ALL of the CO_2 which is ...

... released into the atmosphere, through volcanic activity and fossil fuel burning, ...

... which means that the LEVEL OF CARBON DIOXIDE CONTINUES TO RISE!!

Sedimentary Rocks

At the surface of the Earth SEDIMENTARY ROCKS exist mainly in LAYERS ...

... where the younger sedimentary rocks USUALLY lie on top of older rocks.

A typical cross-section could look like this ...

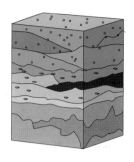

AGE OF ROCK INCREASES

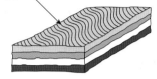

Ripple marks

Examination of the sediments can provide evidence of how they were formed.

• Layers are formed due to the deposition of the sediments at interrupted intervals.
• Ripple marks may be found due to the movement of currents or waves.

However, sedimentary rock layers are often found ...

| ... TILTED | ... FOLDED | ... FRACTURED | ... TURNED UPSIDE DOWN. |

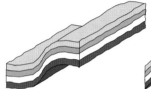 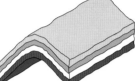 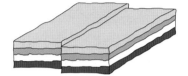 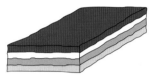

All this shows ...

• ... that the EARTH'S CRUST HAS BEEN SUBJECTED TO VERY LARGE FORCES, ...
• ... to cause this movement of the sedimentary rock layers, and that it is very UNSTABLE!

Forming Mountain Ranges

The Earth's lithosphere ie. the crust and the upper part of the mantle ...

... is 'cracked' into several large pieces called tectonic plates.

These plates move slowly (a few cm per year) ...

... and mountain ranges can form where these plates collide.

When this happens continental crust ie. the crust which forms land ...

... is forced upwards at the point of impact ...

... and SEDIMENTARY ROCKS in the continental crust ...

... are subjected to intense PRESSURE and HIGH TEMPERATURE.

This causes them to change structure ...

... and become METAMORPHIC rocks, ...

... eg. limestone may change into marble.

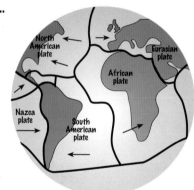

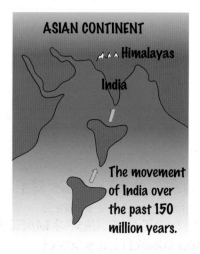

The movement of India over the past 150 million years.

This movement of the crust causes mountain ranges to form very slowly over millions of years. An example of this is where the continental crust which is India, has collided with the Asian crust, to form the Himalayas. These mountains are still being forced upwards as the two plates pile into each other but of course, they are simultaneously being worn away due to weathering and erosion.

Limestone is a SEDIMENTARY ROCK ...
... which consists mainly of CALCIUM CARBONATE.
It is cheap ...
     ... easy to obtain ...
         ... and has many uses:

1. Neutralising Agent

- Excess ACIDITY of soils can cause crop failure.
  - Alkalis can be 'washed out' by acid rain.
    - Powdered limestone can correct this ...
      - ... but it works quite slowly.
- However, when CALCIUM CARBONATE is heated in a kiln...
... a THERMAL DECOMPOSITION reaction takes place ...
... and the calcium carbonate breaks down into the more ...
... simple substances, CALCIUM OXIDE (QUICKLIME) and carbon dioxide.

> **NB**
> Other carbonates behave very similarly when they are heated.

CALCIUM CARBONATE   —HEAT→   CALCIUM OXIDE   +   CARBON DIOXIDE
(limestone)   (quicklime)

- This can then be 'SLAKED' with water to produce CALCIUM HYDROXIDE (SLAKED LIME).

CALCIUM OXIDE   —WATER→   CALCIUM HYDROXIDE
(quicklime)   (slaked lime)

- This, being a HYDROXIDE, is quite strongly ALKALINE ...
  - ... and so can neutralise soils and lakes much faster than just using powdered limestone.

2. Building Material

- Can be QUARRIED and cut ...
  - ... into BLOCKS, and used directly ...
    - ... to build WALLS of houses, ...
      - ... in regions where it is plentiful!
        - It is badly affected by ACID RAIN, ...
          - ... but this takes a long time.

3. Glass Making

- Glass is made by mixing ...
  - ... LIMESTONE, SAND and ...
    - ... SODA (sodium carbonate) ...
      - ... and heating the mixture until it melts.
        - When cool, it is TRANSPARENT.

LIMESTONE   +   SAND   +   SODA   —HEAT→   GLASS

4. Cement Making

CEMENT

- Powdered limestone and powdered CLAY ...
  - ... are roasted in a ROTARY KILN, ...
    - ... to produce dry cement.
      - When the cement is mixed with ...
        - ...WATER, SAND and GRAVEL (crushed rock) ...
          - ... a slow reaction takes place where ...
            - ... a HARD, STONE-LIKE BUILDING MATERIAL, ...
              - ... called CONCRETE, is produced.

Formation Of Crude Oil

- Crude oil, coal and natural gas are FOSSIL FUELS.
- These are fuels which have formed over MILLIONS of years ...
- ... by the action of HEAT and PRESSURE, in the absence of oxygen,
- ... on ORGANIC material from ANIMALS and PLANTS.
- This material gets trapped by layers of sedimentary rock.

Crude oil and natural gas were formed from animals that lived in the sea.

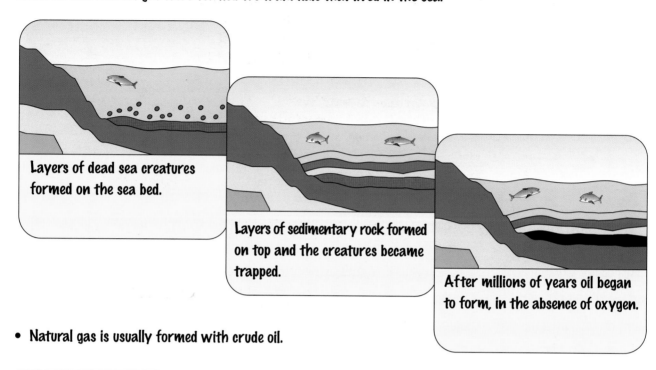

Layers of dead sea creatures formed on the sea bed.

Layers of sedimentary rock formed on top and the creatures became trapped.

After millions of years oil began to form, in the absence of oxygen.

- Natural gas is usually formed with crude oil.

What Crude Oil Is

- Crude oil is a mixture of compounds most of which ...
- ... are MOLECULES made up of CARBON and HYDROGEN atoms only, called HYDROCARBONS.

These hydrocarbon molecules vary in size. This affects their properties.

The LARGER the HYDROCARBON
ie. the greater the number of carbon atoms in a molecule:

1. The LESS EASILY IT FLOWS ...
... ie. the more viscous it is.

2. The LESS EASILY IT IGNITES ...
... ie. the less flammable it is.

3. The LESS VOLATILE IT IS ...
... ie. it doesn't vaporise as easily.

4. The HIGHER ITS BOILING POINT.

Because a mixture consists of two or more elements or compounds, which aren't chemically combined together, the properties of the substances in the mixture remain unchanged and specific to that substance. This makes it possible to separate the substances in a mixture by physical methods such as DISTILLATION. (See next page)

CRUDE OIL II – Fractional Distillation And Cracking ● Changing Materials I

Fractional Distillation Of Crude Oil

Crude oil on its own isn't a great deal of use. However, since crude oil is a mixture of hydrocarbons which aren't chemically combined together, the properties of the hydrocarbons in crude oil remain unchanged and specific. This makes it possible to separate the hydrocarbons into their individual parts, or FRACTIONS, by FRACTIONAL DISTILLATION.

- The oil is evaporated by heating and then allowed to CONDENSE ...
    - ... at a RANGE OF DIFFERENT TEMPERATURES where it forms FRACTIONS.
        - Each of these fractions contain hydrocarbon molecules ...
            - ... with a SIMILAR NUMBER OF CARBON ATOMS.
                - This is done in a FRACTIONATING COLUMN.

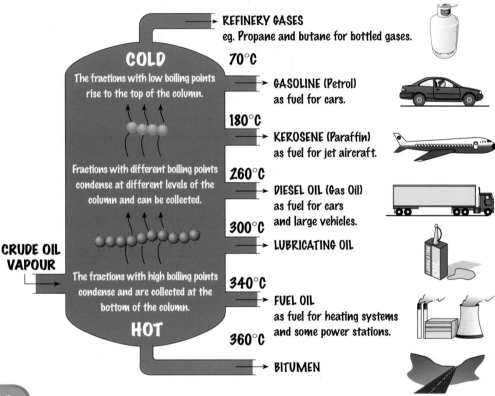

Cracking

Because the SHORTER CHAIN HYDROCARBONS release energy more quickly by BURNING, there is a greater demand for them as fuels. Therefore LONGER CHAIN HYDROCARBONS are 'CRACKED' or broken down into shorter chains.
This is done by heating them until they vaporise; the vapour is then passed over a heated catalyst, ...
... where a THERMAL DECOMPOSITION reaction takes place.
In the laboratory, CRACKING can be carried out using the following apparatus ...

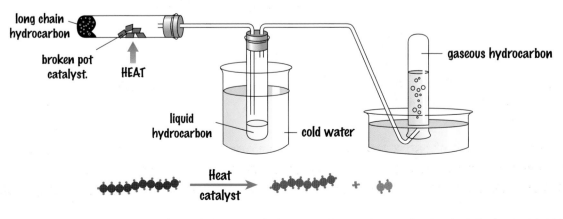

The products of cracking are used ....

.... As Fuels

When a fuel burns, **WASTE PRODUCTS** are released into the atmosphere. Most fuels contain carbon and/or hydrogen and possibly even sulphur. The waste product produced depends on which element is present in the fuel.

If we burn methane which is made up of **CARBON** and **HYDROGEN** ...

CARBON DIOXIDE

WATER VAPOUR

METHANE + OXYGEN $\longrightarrow$ CARBON DIOXIDE + WATER VAPOUR
(an oxide of hydrogen)

$$CH_{4(g)} + 2O_{2(g)} \longrightarrow CO_{2(g)} + 2H_2O_{(l)}$$

.... and if we burn a fuel that contains **SULPHUR** ....

SULPHUR + OXYGEN $\longrightarrow$ SULPHUR DIOXIDE

$$S_{(s)} + O_{2(g)} \longrightarrow SO_{2(g)}$$

However, burning fuels does have an effect on the environment ...

1 Carbon dioxide is one of the 'GREENHOUSE GASES'. Light from the Sun passes through the atmosphere and reaches the Earth, warming it up. The Earth, in return, radiates this heat energy back into **SPACE. CARBON DIOXIDE** in the atmosphere helps to trap some of this energy which keeps the planet warm. Too much carbon dioxide however, leads to too much heat being retained. This is **GLOBAL WARMING**.

2 Sulphur dioxide reacts with water vapour in the atmosphere to produce **ACID RAIN** which causes lakes and rivers to become so acidic that plants and animals cannot survive. It also causes erosion damage to stone and metalwork of buildings.

.... To Make Plastics (polymers)

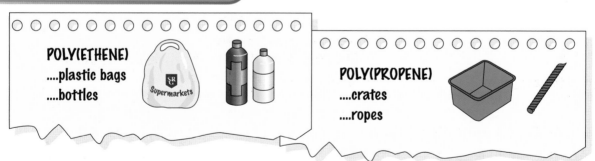

POLY(ETHENE)
....plastic bags
....bottles

Supermarkets

POLY(PROPENE)
....crates
....ropes

Because plastic is such a convenient material we do tend to produce a large amount of plastic waste. There are various ways of disposing of plastics, unfortunately some of them have consequent effects on the environment.

1 <u>Use of landfill sites</u>

The problem with most plastics is that they are non-biodegradable. Microorganisms have no effect on them; they will not decompose and rot away. The use of landfill sites simply means that plastic waste builds up. However research is being carried out on the development of biodegradable plastics.

2 <u>Burning</u>

Burning plastics produces air pollution. The production of carbon dioxide contributes to the greenhouse effect which results in global warming. Some plastics cannot be burned at all as they produce toxic fumes.

Alkanes - Saturated Hydrocarbons

The 'SPINE' of a HYDROCARBON is made up of a chain of CARBON ATOMS.
- When these are joined together by single covalent carbon—carbon bonds ...
- ... we say the HYDROCARBON is SATURATED and it is known as an ALKANE.

To put it simply ...

Hydrogen atoms can make ...
... 1 BOND EACH

Carbon atoms can make ...
... 4 BONDS EACH

The simplest alkane, METHANE, is made up of ...
... 4 HYDROGEN ATOMS and 1 CARBON ATOM.

CH_4

A more convenient way of representing alkanes is as follows ...

METHANE, CH_4

ETHANE, C_2H_6

PROPANE, C_3H_8

- ALL THE CARBON ATOMS ARE LINKED TO 4 OTHER ATOMS.
- THEY ARE ALL 'FULLY OCCUPIED' OR SATURATED.
- ALL THE BONDS ARE SINGLE COVALENT BONDS.

Because all their bonds are 'occupied' they are fairly UNREACTIVE, although they do burn well.

Alkenes - Unsaturated Hydrocarbons

- Carbon atoms can also form DOUBLE COVALENT BONDS with other atoms, and ...
... amongst the products of cracking are HYDROCARBON MOLECULES which have ...
... at least ONE DOUBLE COVALENT BOND.

We say that the HYDROCARBON is UNSATURATED and it is known as an ALKENE.

The simplest alkene is ETHENE, C_2H_4 which ...

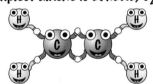

... is made up of 4 HYDROGEN ATOMS ...
... and 2 CARBON ATOMS.
As you can see ethene contains ...
... ONE DOUBLE CARBON=CARBON COVALENT BOND.

Yet again, there is a convenient way of representing alkenes ...

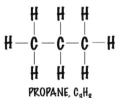

ETHENE, C_2H_4

PROPENE, C_3H_6

- NOT ALL THE CARBON ATOMS ARE LINKED TO 4 OTHER ATOMS.
- THEY ARE NOT ALL 'FULLY OCCUPIED' ie. THEY ARE UNSATURATED.
- A DOUBLE BOND IS PRESENT.

Because of this DOUBLE BOND (=) the ALKENES have the potential to join with other atoms and so they are REACTIVE. This makes them useful for making other molecules, especially POLYMERS.

Polymers are very large molecules which are formed when the small alkene molecules above, called MONOMERS, join together. This process is known as POLYMERISATION.

Test For An Alkene

Alkenes will DECOLOURISE BROMINE WATER as the ALKENE REACTS WITH IT.

eg. **Ethene** + **Bromine Water** ➡ **COLOURLESS SOLUTION**
(colourless)   (yellow-brown)

Monomers To Polymers

One of the important uses of the alkenes which are produced during cracking, is the production of POLYMERS;...
... these are LONG CHAIN MOLECULES, some of which make up PLASTICS.

Because ALKENES are UNSATURATED, they are very good at joining together and when they do so without producing another substance, we call this ADDITION POLYMERISATION.

eg. the formation of poly(ethene) from ethene.

The small alkene molecules are called MONOMERS.

Their double bonds are easily broken.

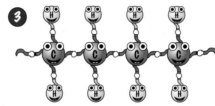

... large numbers of molecules can therefore be joined in this way.

> The resulting long chain molecule is a POLYMER - in this case POLY(ETHENE) ... often called POLYTHENE

A more convenient form of representing addition polymerisation is ...

$$H_2C=CH_2 + H_2C=CH_2 + H_2C=CH_2 + \text{thousands more} \longrightarrow$$

ethene monomers (unsaturated)

$$H-CH_2-CH_2-CH_2-CH_2-CH_2- \cdots \text{and on and on ...}$$

poly(ethene) polymer (saturated)

General Formula For Addition Polymerisation

This can be applied to any ADDITION POLYMERISATION ...
... to represent the formation of a simple addition polymer.

$$n\left(C=C\right) \longrightarrow \left(-C-C-\right)_n$$

... where 'n' is a very large number.

For example, if we take ...

$$n\left(\begin{array}{cc} H & CH_3 \\ C & = & C \\ H & H \end{array}\right) \longrightarrow \left(\begin{array}{cc} H & CH_3 \\ -C & - & C- \\ H & H \end{array}\right)_n$$

... 'n' molecules of propene to produce poly(propene), which is used to make crates and ropes.

THE EARTH'S ATMOSPHERE

HOW IT EVOLVED ...

Volcanic activity releases CO_2 and methane and ammonia.

Green plants evolve reducing CO_2 and increasing O_2

Oxygen hating microbes killed off.

Oxygen much increased.

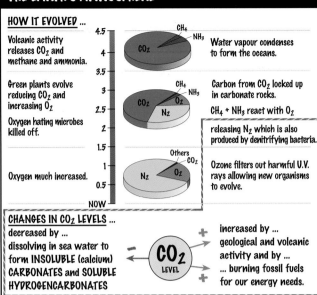

Water vapour condenses to form the oceans.

Carbon from CO_2 locked up in carbonate rocks.

$CH_4 + NH_3$ react with O_2 releasing N_2 which is also produced by denitrifying bacteria.

Ozone filters out harmful U.V. rays allowing new organisms to evolve.

CHANGES IN CO_2 LEVELS ...

decreased by ...
dissolving in sea water to form INSOLUBLE (calcium) CARBONATES and SOLUBLE HYDROGENCARBONATES

CO_2 LEVEL

increased by ...
geological and volcanic activity and by ...
... burning fossil fuels for our energy needs.

SEDIMENTARY AND METAMORPHIC ROCKS

SEDIMENTARY ROCKS

AGE OF ROCK INCREASES

- Sedimentary rocks exist mainly in layers.
- Younger rocks are normally on top of older rocks. Rocks may be ...

... TILTED   ... FOLDED   ... FRACTURED   ... TURNED UPSIDE DOWN.

Examination of the sediments can provide evidence of how they were formed.
- Layers are formed due to the deposition of the sediments at interrupted intervals.
- Ripple marks may be found due to the movement of currents or waves.

FORMING MOUNTAIN RANGES

- Earth's lithosphere is cracked into several large pieces called tectonic plates which move slowly.
- When plates collide continental crust is forced upwards and sedimentary rocks are subjected to intense pressure and high temperatures causing them to change structure to become metamorphic rocks.

Himalayas
The movement of India over the past 150 million years.

- This movement of the crust causes mountain ranges to form slowly over millions of years eg. Himalayas.

LIMESTONE

LIMESTONE ... is made mainly of CALCIUM CARBONATE.

- It can be used as a NEUTRALISING AGENT either directly or as CALCIUM HYDROXIDE

CALCIUM CARBONATE $\xrightarrow{HEAT}$ CALCIUM OXIDE + CARBON DIOXIDE
(limestone)   (quicklime)

This is an example of a THERMAL DECOMPOSITION reaction.

The calcium oxide can then be 'slaked' with water to produce calcium hydroxide (slaked lime).

CALCIUM OXIDE $\xrightarrow{WATER}$ CALCIUM HYDROXIDE
(quicklime)   (slaked lime)

This, being a hydroxide, is quite strongly alkaline and so can neutralise soils and lakes much faster than using just powdered limestone.

- It can be used as a BUILDING MATERIAL where it is cut into blocks to build walls of houses etc.

However, it is affected by acid rain.

- It is used in GLASS MAKING.

LIMESTONE + SAND + SODA $\xrightarrow{HEAT}$ GLASS

- It is used to make CEMENT where powdered limestone and powdered clay are roasted in a rotary kiln to produce dry cement.

CRUDE OIL AND FRACTIONAL DISTILLATION

INTRODUCTION TO CRUDE OIL ... formed by HEAT and PRESSURE in the ABSENCE of OXYGEN on ORGANIC MATERIAL trapped beneath layers of sedimentary rocks for millions of years.

- Crude oil is a mixture of compounds most of which are made up of CARBON and HYDROGEN atoms only, called HYDROCARBONS.

The larger the hydrocarbon molecule ...
- ... the LESS EASILY IT FLOWS.
- ... the LESS EASILY IT IGNITES.
- ... the LESS VOLATILE IT IS.
- ... the HIGHER ITS BOILING POINT.

This mixture can be separated by DISTILLATION.

FRACTIONAL DISTILLATION ...

- The crude oil is heated and allowed to CONDENSE at a RANGE OF DIFFERENT TEMPERATURES.
- The 'fractions' formed contain HYDROCARBON molecules with a similar number of carbon atoms.
- This is done in a fractionating column, shown opposite.

REFINERY GASES 70°C
GASOLINE 180°C
KEROSENE 260°C
DIESEL OIL 300°C
LUBRICATING OIL 340°C
FUEL OIL
CRUDE OIL VAPOUR 360°C
BITUMEN

CRACKING

CRACKING ...

- Shorter chain hydrocarbons are in greater demand because they release ENERGY QUICKLY.
- Long chain hydrocarbons are therefore 'CRACKED' into shorter chains by passing their vapour over a heated catalyst causing THERMAL DECOMPOSITION.

long chain hydrocarbon
broken pot catalyst
HEAT
liquid hydrocarbon
gaseous hydrocarbon

The products of cracking are used ...

1. ... as FUELS

METHANE + OXYGEN $\longrightarrow$ CARBON DIOXIDE + WATER VAPOUR
SULPHUR + OXYGEN $\longrightarrow$ SULPHUR DIOXIDE

- Carbon dioxide is a 'greenhouse gas' where the production of too much CO_2 results in the Earth retaining too much heat energy resulting in global warming.
- Sulphur dioxide reacts with water vapour to produce acid rain.

2. ... to make PLASTICS

POLY(ETHENE) ... plastic bags ... bottles
POLY(PROPENE) ... crates ... ropes

- Disposal of plastics is a problem as most of them are non-biodegradable. The use of landfill sites results in the build up of plastic waste. Burning them is not the solution either as CO_2 is produced and some plastics produce toxic fumes when burned.

ALKANES, ALKENES AND ADDITION POLYMERISATION

ALKANES ... are 'saturated' hydrocarbons in which the carbon atoms are joined together by SINGLE COVALENT BONDS.

METHANE, CH_4 ETHANE, C_2H_6 PROPANE, C_3H_8

ALKENES ... are 'unsaturated' hydrocarbons in which there is at least one DOUBLE COVALENT BOND between the carbon atoms.

ETHENE, C_2H_4 PROPENE, C_3H_6

They are reactive because the double bond allows them to join with other molecules to form POLYMERS. Alkenes are identified by decolourising BROMINE WATER.

ADDITION POLYMERISATION ... is when alkene monomers join together to form a polymer and no other substance eg. lots of ETHENE molecules join up to form POLY(ETHENE).

The general formula is ...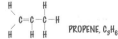

Plastics are polymers and made in this way.

1. The early atmosphere of the Earth was made up mainly of water vapour and three other gases.
   a) Name these gases.
   b) As the first green plants evolved which gas did they take in and which gas did they give out?
   c) Name TWO sources which produced nitrogen to be released into the atmosphere.
   d) What effect did ozone have on the evolution of new living organisms?

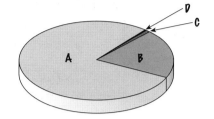

2. The pie chart opposite shows the composition of the atmosphere.
   a) Name 'A', 'B', 'C' and 'D'.
   b) What else may also be present in varying small quantities?

3. a) Explain how volcanic activity and the burning of fossil fuels increase the level of carbon dioxide in the atmosphere.
   b) In what way does sea water help to control the amount of carbon dioxide in the atmosphere?

4. a) Why do sedimentary rocks exist mainly in layers?
   b) The diagrams below show how sedimentary rocks are often found.

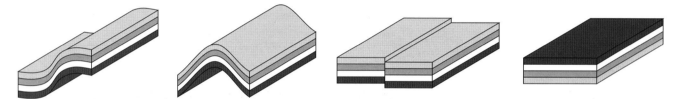

   What do these diagrams show about the Earth's crust?

5. a) What is the lithosphere?
   b) What can form when tectonic plates collide?
   c) What happens to continental crust when plates collide?
   d) Explain how metamorphic rocks form.
   e) Explain how the Himalayas formed.

6. a) Which type of rock is limestone?
   b) Explain, using word equations, how slaked lime is formed.
   c) Why is slaked lime used in preference to powdered limestone as a neutralisation agent?
   d) What disadvantage is there in using limestone as a building material?
   e) How is glass made?
   f) What is cement?

7. Fill in the spaces using the following words.
   SEDIMENTARY, PRESSURE, ORGANIC, SEA, ANIMALS, OXYGEN, PLANTS, HEAT

   Fossil fuels were formed over millions of years from the _____ material of _____ and

   _____ by the action of _____ and _____ in the absence of _____ .

   This material gets trapped by layers of _____ rock. Crude oil and natural gas were formed from

   animals that lived in the _____ .

8. The diagram opposite shows the different fractions of crude oil.
   a) Name the process that takes place to obtain the different fractions.
   b) Name the TWO fractions 'A' and 'B'.
   c) All the fractions contain TWO elements. Name these elements.

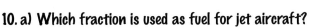
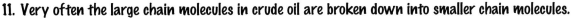

9. Fuel oil has a higher boiling point than diesel oil.
   a) Which of these fuels is more viscous? Explain your answer.
   b) Which of these fuels is less volatile? Explain your answer.
   c) Which of these fuels is the more flammable? Explain your answer.

10. a) Which fraction is used as fuel for jet aircraft?
    b) Which fraction is used for making roads?
    c) Which fraction(s) is used as fuel for cars?

11. Very often the large chain molecules in crude oil are broken down into smaller chain molecules.
    a) What is the process called?
    b) Why are the smaller chain molecules more useful than the larger chain molecules?
    c) The diagram below shows how the process above can be carried out in the laboratory.

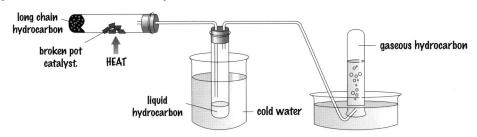

    (i) A thermal decomposition reaction takes place in the process above. What does this mean?
    (ii) What is the purpose of the broken pot catalyst?

12. Natural gas is made up mainly of Methane which contains the elements Carbon and Hydrogen only.
    If Methane is burned ...
    a) which gas from the atmosphere reacts with methane?
    b) what are the TWO waste products formed during the burning?
    c) which one of the waste products turns limewater milky?

13. a) Name ONE gas which is associated with global warming.
    b) Name TWO gases which are associated with acid rain.
    c) Name TWO affects of acid rain.

14. a) Name two plastics.
    b) Most plastics are non-biodegradable. Why is this a problem when they are disposed of in landfill sites?
    c) Disposing of plastics by burning them is no solution either. Explain why.

15. A molecule of methane has the following structure ...

    a) Draw the structure of (i) ethane and (ii) propane.
    b) Methane, ethane and propane are all 'saturated' hydrocarbons. Explain what this means.

16. a) What are alkenes?
    b) Draw a diagram of the structure of a molecule of ethene.
    c) Describe very simply a test that can distinguish an alkene from an alkane.
    d) Ethene can be polymerised to form which polymer?
    e) Explain why ethane cannot be polymerised whereas ethene can.

Reaction Of Metals With Oxygen

• Metals which react with OXYGEN from the AIR form METAL OXIDES.

METAL + OXYGEN ⟶ METAL OXIDE

• Some metals react more vigorously than others. If we were to heat four different metals in air ...

| SODIUM ... | MAGNESIUM ... | COPPER ... | SILVER ... |

... BURNS VERY EASILY   ... BURNS BRIGHTLY   ... SLOW REACTION   ... NO REACTION

Reaction Of Metals With Water

• Metals which react with WATER form either METAL HYDROXIDES or METAL OXIDES and HYDROGEN.

METAL + WATER ⟶ METAL HYDROXIDE or METAL OXIDE + HYDROGEN

• Yet again some metals react more vigorously than others. If we were to add four different metals to water ...

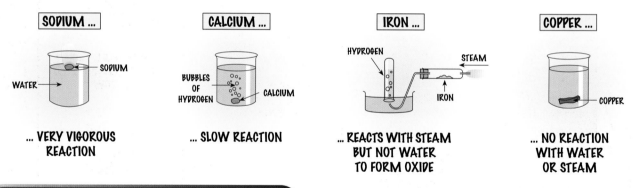

... VERY VIGOROUS REACTION   ... SLOW REACTION   ... REACTS WITH STEAM BUT NOT WATER TO FORM OXIDE   ... NO REACTION WITH WATER OR STEAM

Reaction Of Metals With Dilute Acids

• Metals which react with DILUTE ACID form a METAL 'SALT' and HYDROGEN. A 'SALT' is a word used to describe ANY METAL COMPOUND made when a reaction takes place between a metal and an acid.

METAL + ACID ⟶ SALT + HYDROGEN

• However some metals react more vigorously than others. If we were to add four different metals to acid ...

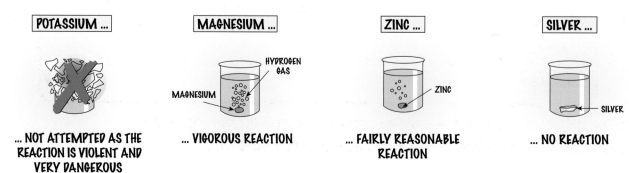

... NOT ATTEMPTED AS THE REACTION IS VIOLENT AND VERY DANGEROUS   ... VIGOROUS REACTION   ... FAIRLY REASONABLE REACTION   ... NO REACTION

The REACTIVITY SERIES places metals in order of their reactivity based on how vigorously they react with ...

... ❶ OXYGEN (or AIR)

... ❷ WATER

... ❸ DILUTE ACID

The more vigorously a metal reacts, the higher up the reactivity series it is.

ELEMENT	REACTION WITH OXYGEN (AIR)	REACTION WITH WATER	REACTION WITH DILUTE ACID
POTASSIUM		HYDROGEN GAS / SODIUM / WATER	
SODIUM	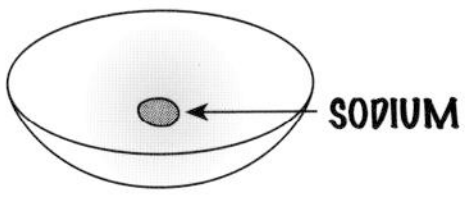 SODIUM — BURN BRIGHTLY WHEN HEATED TO FORM OXIDE	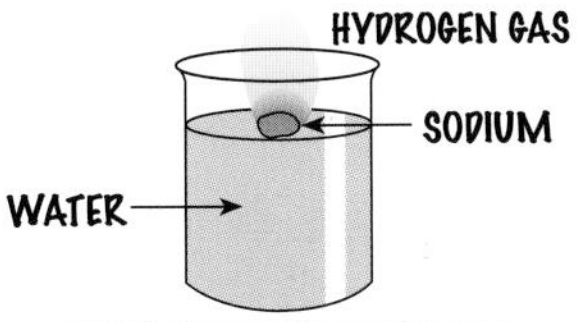 VERY VIGOROUS REACTION IN COLD WATER FORMS HYDROXIDE	 VIOLENT REACTION AND VERY DANGEROUS
CALCIUM	MAGNESIUM / BUNSEN BURNER	BUBBLES OF HYDROGEN / CALCIUM	
MAGNESIUM	 BURN BRIGHTLY IN AIR WHEN HEATED TO FORM OXIDE	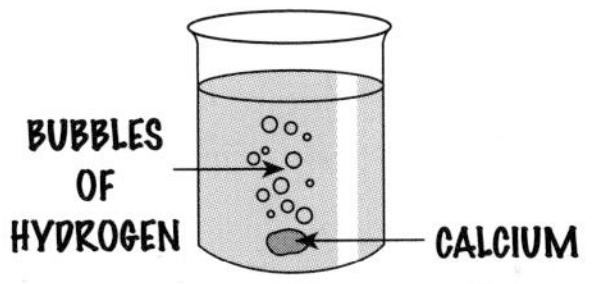 SLOW REACTION IN COLD WATER TO FORM HYDROXIDE	
ALUMINIUM			HYDROGEN GAS
CARBON			
ZINC		HYDROGEN / STEAM / IRON	MAGNESIUM
IRON	COPPER / BUNSEN BURNER	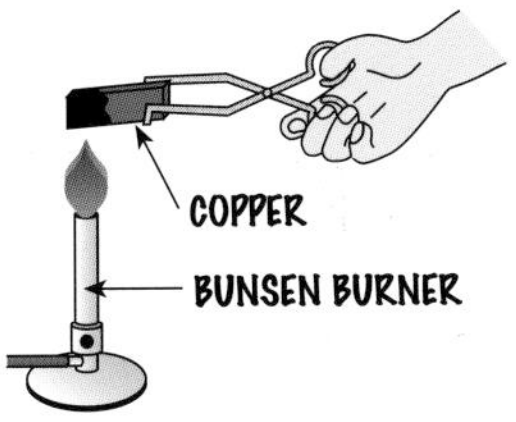 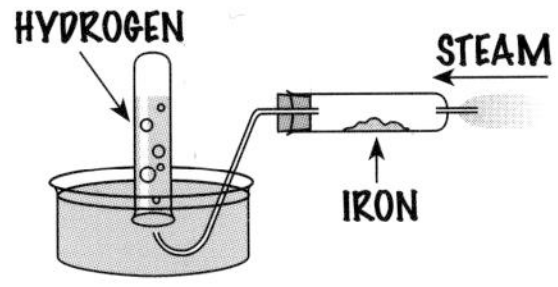 REACTS WITH STEAM, BUT NOT WATER, TO FORM OXIDE	REASONABLE REACTION WHICH DECREASES AS WE GO DOWN
TIN			IRON
LEAD	SLOW REACTION WHEN HEATED TO FORM OXIDE		
HYDROGEN			
COPPER			
SILVER		COPPER	
GOLD	SILVER / BUNSEN BURNER / NO REACTION	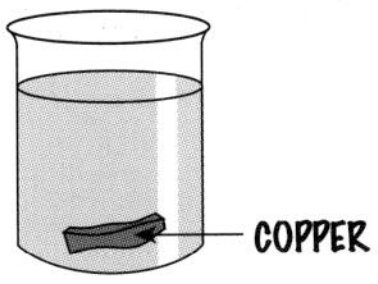 NO REACTION WITH WATER OR STEAM	GOLD / NO REACTION
PLATINUM			

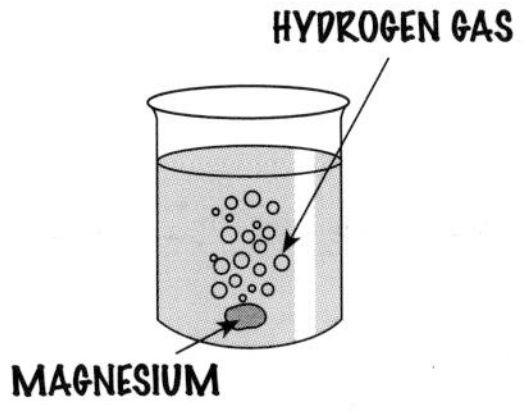

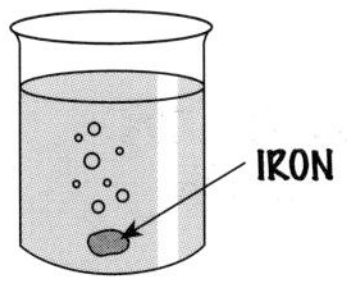

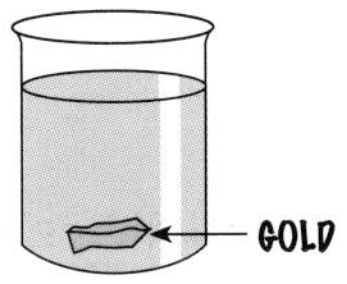

VERY REACTIVE / QUITE REACTIVE / NOT SO REACTIVE / NOT REACTIVE AT ALL

INCREASING REACTIVITY

Carbon and hydrogen, although non-metals, are often shown in the reactivity series because they can displace less reactive metals from their oxides (see P.31).

A DISPLACEMENT REACTION is one in which a MORE REACTIVE METAL DISPLACES a LESS REACTIVE METAL from a compound. In other words a metal higher up in the reactivity series will 'push out' a metal lower in the Series.

- If we put an IRON nail into a beaker of COPPER SULPHATE solution ...

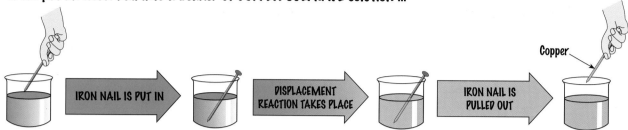

... then a DISPLACEMENT REACTION OCCURS because IRON is higher ...
... in the REACTIVITY SERIES than COPPER.

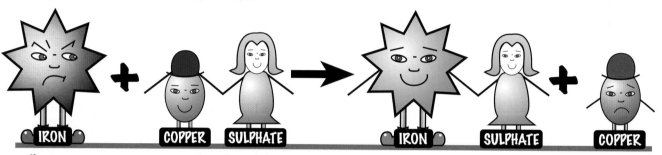

| The more REACTIVE iron ... | ... takes the sulphate from the copper ... | ... to form iron sulphate ... | ... and copper. |

IRON + COPPER SULPHATE ⟶ IRON SULPHATE + COPPER

There is one simple rule to remember:

> A METAL HIGHER UP THE REACTIVITY SERIES (MORE REACTIVE) WILL DISPLACE
> A LESS REACTIVE METAL FROM ITS COMPOUND.

Similarly if a mixture of aluminium powder and iron oxide is heated, an extremely vigorous displacement reaction occurs, because ...

MAGNESIUM RIBBON 'FUSE'

ALUMINIUM POWDER AND IRON OXIDE

SMALL PLUG OF IRON REMAINS

... aluminium is higher in the reactivity series than iron.

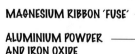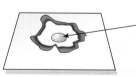
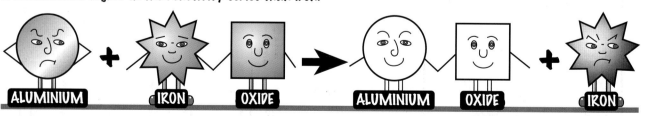

| The more REACTIVE aluminium ... | ... takes the oxygen from the iron ... | ... to form aluminium oxide ... | ... and iron. |

ALUMINIUM + IRON OXIDE ⟶ ALUMINIUM OXIDE + IRON

Example No. 1 ZINC + COPPER SULPHATE SOLUTION

ZINC + COPPER SULPHATE ⟶ ZINC SULPHATE + COPPER

Yes! Zinc is higher in the reactivity series so it displaces the copper forming zinc sulphate.

POTASSIUM
SODIUM
CALCIUM
MAGNESIUM
ALUMINIUM
CARBON
ZINC
IRON
TIN
LEAD
HYDROGEN
COPPER
SILVER
GOLD
PLATINUM

Example No. 2 COPPER + LEAD NITRATE SOLUTION

COPPER + LEAD NITRATE ⟶ LEAD NITRATE + COPPER

No! Copper is lower in the 'series' than lead so no reaction takes place.

POTASSIUM
SODIUM
CALCIUM
MAGNESIUM
ALUMINIUM
CARBON
ZINC
IRON
TIN
LEAD
HYDROGEN
COPPER
SILVER
GOLD
PLATINUM

Example No. 3 MAGNESIUM + COPPER SULPHATE SOLUTION

MAGNESIUM + COPPER SULPHATE ⟶ MAGNESIUM SULPHATE + COPPER

Yes! Magnesium is higher in the 'series' so it displaces the copper forming magnesium sulphate.

POTASSIUM
SODIUM
CALCIUM
MAGNESIUM
ALUMINIUM
CARBON
ZINC
IRON
TIN
LEAD
HYDROGEN
COPPER
SILVER
GOLD
PLATINUM

Example No. 4 SILVER + IRON SULPHATE SOLUTION

SILVER + IRON SULPHATE ⟶ IRON SULPHATE + SILVER

No! Silver is lower in the 'series' than iron so no reaction takes place.

POTASSIUM
SODIUM
CALCIUM
MAGNESIUM
ALUMINIUM
CARBON
ZINC
IRON
TIN
LEAD
HYDROGEN
COPPER
SILVER
GOLD
PLATINUM

Displacement Reactions Involving Carbon And Hydrogen

Although they are non-metals, carbon and hydrogen often appear in the reactivity series because of their ability to displace less reactive METALS from their OXIDES (See P.29).

Example No. 1 CARBON + LEAD OXIDE

CARBON + LEAD OXIDE ⟶ LEAD + CARBON DIOXIDE

Yes! Carbon is higher in the 'series' so it displaces the lead.
This reaction needs heat for it to occur.

POTASSIUM
SODIUM
CALCIUM
MAGNESIUM
ALUMINIUM
CARBON
ZINC
IRON
TIN
LEAD
HYDROGEN
COPPER
SILVER
GOLD
PLATINUM

Example No. 2 HYDROGEN + COPPER OXIDE

POTASSIUM
SODIUM
CALCIUM
MAGNESIUM
ALUMINIUM
CARBON
ZINC
IRON
TIN
LEAD
HYDROGEN
COPPER
SILVER
GOLD
PLATINUM

HYDROGEN + COPPER OXIDE ⟶ COPPER + WATER

Yes! Hydrogen is higher in the 'series', so it displaces the copper.
This reaction needs heat for it to occur.

Metal Ores

- The Earth's crust contains many naturally occurring elements and compounds called MINERALS.
- A METAL ORE is a mineral or mixture of minerals from which economically viable amounts of pure metal can be extracted.
- Most ores contain either METAL OXIDES or substances which can be easily changed into a METAL OXIDE.
- To extract the metal from a metal oxide the OXYGEN MUST BE REMOVED.
- The removal of OXYGEN is called REDUCTION.

Methods Of Extraction

As we have seen, some metals are more reactive than others. The method of extraction of a metal from its ore depends on its position in the REACTIVITY SERIES. The position of CARBON in this list plays a very important part.

POSITION OF METAL	METHOD OF EXTRACTION	EXAMPLES
POTASSIUM		Electrolysis of aluminium oxide (See P.34)
SODIUM	METALS ABOVE CARBON: Due to the high reactivity of these metals, a large amount of energy is required in a process called ELECTROLYSIS.	
CALCIUM		
MAGNESIUM		
ALUMINIUM		
— CARBON —		
ZINC		Reduction of iron oxide in the blast furnace (See P.33).
IRON		
TIN	METALS BELOW CARBON: These metals can be extracted by HEATING WITH CARBON since carbon is a more reactive element. HOT AIR	
LEAD		
COPPER		
SILVER	METALS AT THE BOTTOM OF THE SERIES: These metals are unreactive and exist naturally (silver can also exist as an ore). They are obtained by physical processes such as panning.	Panning for gold.
GOLD		
PLATINUM		

THE MOST REACTIVE METALS ARE THE MOST DIFFICULT TO EXTRACT FROM THEIR ORES.

THE LEAST REACTIVE METALS ARE THE EASIEST TO EXTRACT.

Extraction Of Iron – The Blast Furnace

Iron is BELOW CARBON in the reactivity series. It is one of the most widely used metals in the world; used for building, transport and everyday objects.
Haematite is the name of the ore from which iron is extracted. It contains IRON OXIDE.

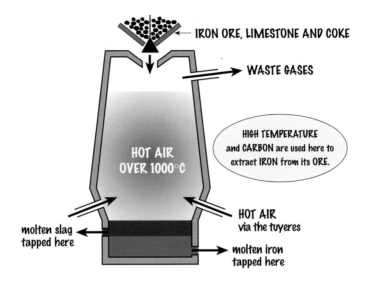

IRON ORE, LIMESTONE AND COKE

WASTE GASES

HIGH TEMPERATURE and CARBON are used here to extract IRON from its ORE.

HOT AIR OVER 1000°C

HOT AIR via the tuyeres

molten slag tapped here

molten iron tapped here

- HAEMATITE (iron ore), limestone and coke (carbon) are fed into the top of the furnace ...
  ... hot air is blasted in at the bottom.

- The CARBON REACTS WITH OXYGEN to form CARBON DIOXIDE and a great deal of heat energy.

$$CARBON \ + \ OXYGEN \longrightarrow CARBON \ DIOXIDE \ + \ HEAT \ ENERGY$$
$$C_{(s)} \ + \ O_{2(g)} \longrightarrow CO_{2(g)}$$

- At these high temperatures the carbon dioxide will react with more carbon to form carbon monoxide.

$$CARBON \ DIOXIDE \ + \ CARBON \longrightarrow CARBON \ MONOXIDE$$
$$CO_{2(g)} \ + \ C_{(s)} \longrightarrow 2CO_{(g)}$$

- CARBON MONOXIDE IS A REDUCING AGENT and will take the oxygen from the iron oxide leaving just iron.
  ie. it 'reduces' the iron oxide to molten iron which flows to the bottom of the furnace where it can be tapped off. Carbon itself is often used to reduce oxides as it is quite high in the reactivity series.
  However, here it is CARBON MONOXIDE which acts as the REDUCING AGENT.

$$IRON \ OXIDE \ + \ CARBON \ MONOXIDE \longrightarrow IRON \ + \ CARBON \ DIOXIDE$$
$$Fe_2O_{3(s)} \ + \ 3CO_{(g)} \longrightarrow 2Fe_{(l)} \ + \ 3CO_{2(g)}$$

- The limestone reacts with impurities, including sand, to form the slag.

Reduction And Oxidation

- The loss of oxygen from an oxide is known as REDUCTION. The IRON (III) OXIDE above is made up of two iron atoms chemically combined with three oxygen atoms. On reacting with carbon monoxide (CO) the iron (III) oxide is reduced to IRON which no longer has any oxygen atoms chemically combined with it.

- The process by which oxygen is added to an element or compound is known as OXIDATION.
  An example above is where carbon monoxide combines with the oxygen from iron oxide to form carbon dioxide.

Extraction Of Aluminium – By Electrolysis

- Aluminium must be obtained from its ore by electrolysis because it is too reactive to be extracted by heating with carbon. (Look at their positions in the reactivity series).
- When ionic substances which are made up of ions are dissolved in WATER or MELTED, ...
    - ... they can be broken down (decomposed) into simpler substances, ...
    - ... by passing an ELECTRIC CURRENT through them.
- This process is called ELECTROLYSIS and depends on +ve and -ve ions being free to move about, which can only happen when the substance is in solution or melted.
- During electrolysis, positively charged ions (eg. metal ions) move to the NEGATIVE ELECTRODE ...
    - ... and negatively charged ions move to the POSITIVE ELECTRODE.
- This can cause gases to be given off, or metals to be deposited at the electrodes.

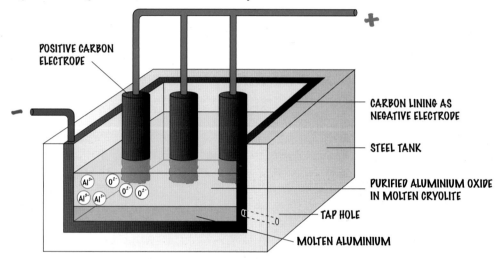

POSITIVE CARBON ELECTRODE

CARBON LINING AS NEGATIVE ELECTRODE

STEEL TANK

PURIFIED ALUMINIUM OXIDE IN MOLTEN CRYOLITE

TAP HOLE

MOLTEN ALUMINIUM

- ALUMINIUM ORE (BAUXITE) is purified to leave aluminium oxide.
- Aluminium oxide is MIXED WITH CRYOLITE (a compound of aluminium) TO LOWER ITS MELTING POINT.
- The aluminium oxide and cryolite mixture is melted ...
    - ... so that the IONS CAN MOVE.
- When a CURRENT passes through the molten mixture ...
- ... AT THE NEGATIVE ELECTRODE ...
- ... POSITIVELY CHARGED ALUMINIUM IONS MOVE TOWARDS IT and ALUMINIUM FORMS and ...
- ... AT THE POSITIVE ELECTRODES ...
- ... NEGATIVELY CHARGED OXIDE IONS MOVE TOWARDS THEM and OXYGEN FORMS.
- This causes the positive electrodes to burn away quickly and they frequently have to be replaced.

━ HIGHER TIER ━

Redox Reactions

During electrolysis ...
- ... at the NEGATIVE ELECTRODE POSITIVELY CHARGED IONS GAIN ELECTRONS.
- This gain of electrons is known as REDUCTION.
- At the POSITIVE ELECTRODE NEGATIVELY CHARGED IONS LOSE ELECTRONS.
- This loss of electrons is known as OXIDATION.
- A chemical reaction where BOTH REDUCTION and OXIDATION occurs is called a REDOX REACTION. It will help you to remember the above if you apply the word 'OILRIG'.

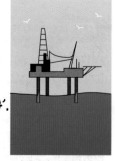

OXIDATION IS LOSS O I L
OF ELECTRONS.

REDUCTION IS GAIN R I G
OF ELECTRONS.

Purification Of Copper By Electrolysis

Copper can easily be extracted by REDUCTION but when it is needed in a pure form it is purified by ELECTROLYSIS.

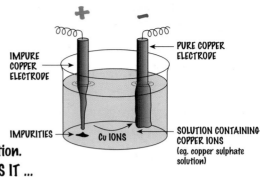

- The POSITIVE ELECTRODE is made of IMPURE COPPER.
- The NEGATIVE ELECTRODE is made of PURE COPPER.
- The solution MUST contain COPPER IONS
- AT THE POSITIVE ELECTRODE COPPER IONS pass into the solution.
- AT THE NEGATIVE ELECTRODE COPPER IONS MOVE TOWARDS IT ...

   ... TO FORM COPPER ATOMS ...

   ... which stick to the pure copper electrode.

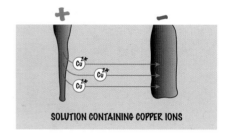

- Consequently the negative electrode gets bigger and bigger as the positive electrode seems to 'dissolve' away to nothing.
- The impurities in the positive electrode simply fall to the bottom as the process takes place.

SOLUTION CONTAINING COPPER IONS

The Rusting Of Iron

When iron reacts with water and oxygen ...

- ... rust (hydrated iron oxide) is formed ...
- ... and this weakens the iron.
- Rusting is an example of an OXIDATION REACTION ...
   ... but it is not very useful to us!

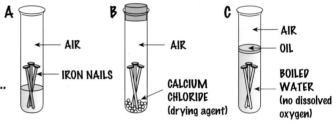

BOTH OXYGEN AND WATER are needed for rusting.
Salt (sodium chloride) can speed up the rate of rusting.

THREE DAYS LATER ...
A - RUST   B - NO RUST   C - NO RUST

Sacrificial Protection

- Iron (or steel) corrodes more quickly than most other transition metals but this can be prevented by connecting the iron to a more reactive metal such as zinc or magnesium.

ZINC BARS ATTACHED TO THE HULL

- The more reactive metal reacts preferentially with the water and oxygen thus preventing it reacting with the iron.
- Zinc bars are attached to the hulls of ships, and magnesium strips to underground steel pipes to prevent corrosion. Only when these have corroded will the iron or steel begin to corrode.

- GALVANISING relies on coating iron objects with zinc. Even if they are scratched they still won't corrode until ALL the zinc has gone.
- Some objects, such as knives and forks, are made from non-rusting alloys such as STAINLESS STEEL which is an alloy containing chromium.

Aluminium – A Special Case

Although aluminium is a quite reactive metal it doesn't oxidise (corrode) as quickly as you would think. This is due to the formation of a thin 'skin' of oxide which forms on the surface and prevents further rusting. It's for this reason that greenhouses don't have to be painted. Aluminium can be made HARDER, STRONGER, and STIFFER, by mixing it with small amounts of other metals (magnesium, titanium) to make alloys.

Production Of Ammonia – The Haber Process

The production of ammonia and nitric acid are intermediate steps in the production of ammonium nitrate fertiliser. Until 1908 nitrogen couldn't be turned into nitrates on a large scale, and the world was quickly running out of fertilisers! Even though air is almost 80% nitrogen!

Fritz Haber showed that ammonia, a COLOURLESS, PUNGENT, ALKALINE GAS could be made on a large scale.

The raw materials are:-
- NITROGEN - from the fractional distillation of liquid air.
- HYDROGEN - from natural gas and steam.

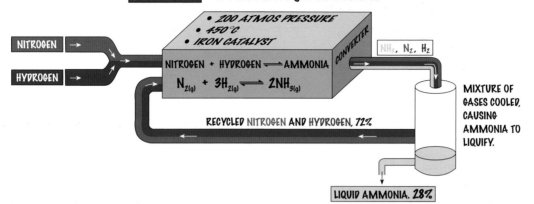

The purified NITROGEN and HYDROGEN are passed over an IRON CATALYST at a temperature of about 450 °C and a pressure of about 200 atmospheres. These reaction conditions are chosen to produce a reasonable yield of ammonia quickly, but even so, only some of the hydrogen and nitrogen react together to form ammonia.

$$NITROGEN + HYDROGEN \rightleftharpoons AMMONIA$$
$$N_{2\,(g)} + 3H_{2\,(g)} \rightleftharpoons 2NH_{3\,(g)}$$

This is an example of a REVERSIBLE reaction: a reaction that can go in both directions, with the ammonia produced breaking back down again to form both nitrogen and hydrogen.

Ammonia Is An Important Chemical

Its main use is in the production of FERTILISERS to increase the nitrogen content of the soil.
Ammonia is also used to produce NITRIC ACID, this process involves two reactions, both of them involving OXYGEN.

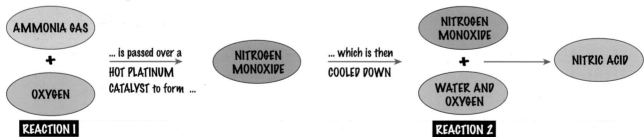

More ammonia can be used to NEUTRALISE the nitric acid to produce AMMONIUM NITRATE - a fertiliser rich in NITROGEN, and sometimes known as 'NITRAM' (nitrate of ammonia).

$$AMMONIA + NITRIC\ ACID \longrightarrow AMMONIUM\ NITRATE$$
$$NH_{3(aq)} + HNO_{3(aq)} \longrightarrow NH_4NO_{3(aq)}$$

The aqueous ammonium nitrate is then evaporated to dryness.
Although nitrogen-based fertilisers are important chemicals, they also create problems ....

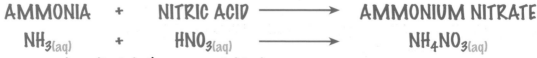

Nitrogen-based fertilisers are important in agriculture ... → ... as they increase the yields of crops. However, nitrates can create problems ... → ... if they find their way into streams, rivers or groundwater, as they can contaminate ... → ... our drinking water.

There is great economic importance attached to getting the MAXIMUM AMOUNT of AMMONIA in the SHORTEST POSSIBLE TIME. This demands a degree of COMPROMISE.

Effect Of Energy Transfer, Rates Of Reaction And Equilibrium Conditions On Reversible Reactions

The manufacture of AMMONIA is a REVERSIBLE REACTION, involving ...
• ENERGY TRANSFERS associated with the breaking and formation of chemical bonds.

$$\boxed{\text{ENDOTHERMIC}} \quad N_{2\,(g)} \;+\; 3H_{2\,(g)} \quad \underset{\text{REVERSE}}{\overset{\text{FORWARD}}{\rightleftharpoons}} \quad 2NH_{3\,(g)} \quad \boxed{\text{EXOTHERMIC}}$$

In a CLOSED SYSTEM, AT EQUILIBRIUM, ...
  • ... there is the SAME RATE OF REACTION IN EACH DIRECTION ...
  • ... but, the RELATIVE AMOUNTS OF THE REACTANTS depend on ...
       ... the CONDITIONS OF THE REACTION.

ENERGY TRANSFERS INVOLVED

Less energy is needed to break the bonds in the nitrogen and hydrogen molecules than is released in the formation of the ammonia molecules.

EFFECT OF TEMPERATURE 1

Because the formation of ammonia is exothermic, ...
... LOW TEMPERATURE WOULD FAVOUR THE PRODUCTION OF AMMONIA. ie. favours the forward reaction ...
... which would increase the yield.

EFFECT OF TEMPERATURE 2

Increasing the temperature increases the rate of reaction equally in both directions, therefore ...
... HIGH TEMPERATURE WOULD MAKE AMMONIA FORM FASTER (and break down faster!)

EFFECT OF PRESSURE

Since four molecules are being changed into two molecules, increasing the pressure favours the smaller volume. Therefore ... HIGH PRESSURE FAVOURS THE PRODUCTION OF AMMONIA, ...
... and increases the yield.

A Compromise Solution

In reality, <u>A LOW TEMPERATURE INCREASES YIELD BUT THE REACTION IS TOO SLOW.</u>
So, a COMPROMISE is reached in the Haber process ...

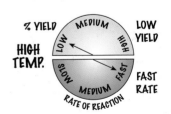

450°C is used as a COMPROMISE SOLUTION.

... while also ...   CONCENTRATION or in this case PRESSURE also has an important role.
  • INCREASING THE PRESSURE, favours the reaction which results in a reduction in volume ...
  • ... and therefore MOVES THE EQUILIBRIUM to the RIGHT ... INCREASING THE YIELD ...
  • ... as the VOLUME OF AMMONIA PRODUCED is LESS ...
  • ... than the TOTAL VOLUME of NITROGEN and HYDROGEN which react to produce it.

In reality, <u>A HIGH PRESSURE INCREASES YIELD BUT THE REACTION IS TOO EXPENSIVE.</u>
So, yet again, a COMPROMISE is reached ...

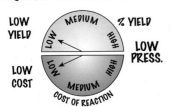

200 ATMOS.PRESS. is used as a COMPROMISE SOLUTION.

REACTIVITY OF METALS

1. OXYGEN   METAL + OXYGEN → METAL OXIDE
e.g. Magnesium + Oxygen ⟶ Magnesium Oxide

2. WATER   METAL + WATER → *METAL HYDROXIDE + HYDROGEN
*(some form oxides)
e.g. Calcium + Water ⟶ Calcium Hydroxide + Hydrogen

3. ACIDS   METAL + ACID → SALT + HYDROGEN
e.g. Zinc + Hydrochloric Acid ⟶ Zinc Chloride + Hydrogen

REACTIVITY SERIES
Depending on how vigorously they react with the above substances, metals (and carbon + hydrogen) can be placed in order ...

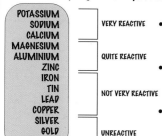

POTASSIUM	VERY REACTIVE
SODIUM	
CALCIUM	
MAGNESIUM	QUITE REACTIVE
ALUMINIUM	
ZINC	
IRON	NOT VERY REACTIVE
TIN	
LEAD	
COPPER	
SILVER	
GOLD	UNREACTIVE
PLATINUM	

- Some reactions such as adding sodium or potassium to acid are dangerous and should <u>not</u> be attempted.
- Carbon and hydrogen, although non-metals, can be placed according to their reactivity.
- This series can then be used to predict which metals will displace other metals from metal compounds.

DISPLACEMENT REACTIONS

'A metal higher up in the reactivity series will displace a less reactive metal from its compound'.

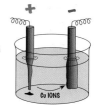

The more REACTIVE iron ... takes the sulphate from the copper ... to form iron sulphate ... and copper.

IRON NAIL IS PUT IN → DISPLACEMENT REACTION TAKES PLACE → IRON NAIL IS PULLED OUT

EXAMPLES OF DISPLACEMENT REACTIONS ...

1. ZINC + COPPER SULPHATE ⟶ ZINC SULPHATE + COPPER ✓
2. COPPER + LEAD NITRATE ⟶ LEAD NITRATE + COPPER ✗
3. MAGNESIUM + COPPER SULPHATE ⟶ MAGNESIUM SULPHATE + COPPER ✓
4. SILVER + IRON SULPHATE ⟶ SILVER + IRON SULPHATE ✗
5. CARBON + LEAD OXIDE ⟶ LEAD + CARBON DIOXIDE ✓
6. HYDROGEN + COPPER OXIDE ⟶ COPPER + WATER ✓
7. ALUMINIUM + IRON OXIDE ⟶ ALUMINIUM OXIDE + IRON. ✓

EXTRACTING METALS

METHODS OF EXTRACTION ...

1. Metals above carbon in the Reactivity Series are extracted by ELECTROLYSIS eg. aluminium.
2. Metals below carbon in the Reactivity Series are extracted by HEATING WITH CARBON eg. iron.
3. Metals at the bottom of the Series are UNREACTIVE and are found naturally eg. gold.

EXTRACTION OF IRON - THE BLAST FURNACE ...

IRON ORE, LIMESTONE AND COKE
WASTE GASES
HOT AIR
HOT AIR via the tuyeres
molten slag tapped here
molten iron tapped here

- The ore, rich in iron oxide is called HAEMATITE.
- With limestone and coke it is fed into the furnace.
- Carbon reacts with oxygen to form carbon dioxide which reacts with more carbon to form carbon monoxide (a reducing agent).

IRON OXIDE + CARBON MONOXIDE ⟶ IRON + CARBON DIOXIDE.

EXTRACTION OF ALUMINIUM - ELECTROLYSIS ...

- Aluminium ore, BAUXITE is mixed with CRYOLITE to lower its melting point.
- At the -ve electrode, Al^{3+} ⟶ Aluminium
- At the +ve electrode, O^{2-} ⟶ Oxygen
  The oxygen causes the electrodes to burn away.

PURIFICATION OF COPPER, CORROSION AND REDOX REACTIONS

PURIFICATION OF COPPER BY ELECTROLYSIS ...
copper, extracted by reduction, can be purified by electrolysis ..

- At the +ve electrode copper ions pass into solution
- At the -ve electrode copper ions become copper atoms and are deposited making the electrode grow bigger.

Cu IONS

SACRIFICIAL PROTECTION ...

this is when a more reactive metal is attached to a less reactive metal in order that it corrodes first leaving the less reactive metal intact. eg. zinc bars are attached to ship's hulls, magnesium strips are stuck to underground pipes and outdoor objects may be GALVANISED using molten zinc.

REDOX REACTIONS ...

during electrolysis, positively charged ions gain electrons at the -ve electrode, while negatively charged ions lose electrons at the +ve electrode.
This is REDUCTION and OXIDATION respectively i.e. a REDOX REACTION.
'OILRIG' = Oxidation is loss of electrons; Reduction is gain of electrons.

PRODUCTION OF AMMONIA

THE HABER PROCESS

- Ammonia is a colourless, pungent, alkaline gas.
  The raw materials for its production are:
- NITROGEN - from the fractional distillation of liquid air.
- HYDROGEN - from natural gas and steam.

Purified nitrogen and hydrogen are passed over an IRON CATALYST at a temp. of 450°C and a pressure of about 200 atmospheres.

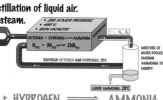

* 200 ATMOS PRESSURE
* 450°C
* IRON CATALYST
NITROGEN + HYDROGEN ⟶ AMMONIA
$N_2 + 3H_2$ ⟶ $2NH_3$
RECYCLED NITROGEN AND HYDROGEN, 72%
MIXTURE OF GASES COOLER CAUSING AMMONIA TO LIQUIFY.
LIQUID AMMONIA 28%

NITROGEN + HYDROGEN ⇌ AMMONIA

NITRIC ACID

AMMONIA GAS + OXYGEN ... is passed over A HOT PLATINUM CATALYST to form ... NITROGEN MONOXIDE ... which is then COOLED DOWN ... NITROGEN MONOXIDE + WATER AND OXYGEN ⟶ NITRIC ACID

REACTION 1   REACTION 2

FERTILISERS

AMMONIA + NITRIC ACID ⟶ AMMONIUM NITRATE

... a fertiliser rich in nitrogen (sometimes known as NITRAM).
- Fertilisers increase the yields of crops, however, if they find their way into streams, rivers or ground water ...
  ... they can contaminate our drinking water.

ECONOMICS OF THE HABER PROCESS

ENDOTHERMIC $N_2 (g)$ + $3H_2 (g)$ FORWARD ⇌ REVERSE $2NH_3 (g)$ EXOTHERMIC

ENERGY TRANSFERS INVOLVED ... less energy is needed to break the bonds in the nitrogen and hydrogen molecules than is released in the formation of the ammonia molecules.

EFFECT OF TEMPERATURE 1 ... because the formation of ammonia is exothermic, LOW TEMPERATURE WOULD FAVOUR THE PRODUCTION OF AMMONIA. ie. favours the forward reaction which would increase the yield.

EFFECT OF TEMPERATURE 2 ... increasing the temperature increases the rate of reaction equally in both directions, therefore HIGH TEMPERATURE WOULD MAKE AMMONIA FORM FASTER (and break down faster!)

EFFECT OF PRESSURE ... since four molecules are being changed into two molecules, increasing the pressure favours the smaller volume. Therefore HIGH PRESSURE FAVOURS THE PRODUCTION OF AMMONIA, and increases the yield.

A COMPROMISE SOLUTION

- A low temperature increases yield but the reaction is too slow.

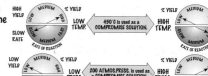

450°C is used as a compromise solution.

- A high pressure increases yield but the reaction is too expensive.

200 ATMOS.PRESS. is used as a COMPROMISE SOLUTION.

SUMMARY QUESTIONS

1. Below are the results of some experiments carried out on four different metals.

METAL	Reaction with Air	Reaction with Water	Reaction with Dilute Acid
A	Burns brightly	Slow reaction	Reasonable reaction with many bubbles of gas produced
B	No reaction	No reaction	Slow reaction with a few bubbles of gas produced
C	No reaction	No reaction	No reaction
D	Burns violently	Very vigorous reaction	Violent reaction

a) Using the results above list the FOUR metals 'A', 'B' 'C' and 'D' in order of reactivity with the most reactive first.

b) The reaction of 'A' with dilute acid produces a gas (i) name the gas (ii) describe a simple laboratory test for this gas.

2. Complete the word equations for the reaction of each of the following metals with either oxygen, water or dilute acid.

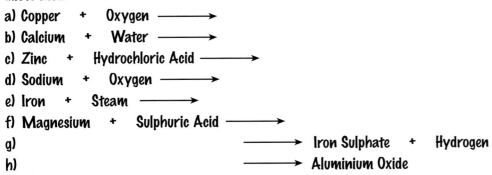

a) Copper + Oxygen ⟶

b) Calcium + Water ⟶

c) Zinc + Hydrochloric Acid ⟶

d) Sodium + Oxygen ⟶

e) Iron + Steam ⟶

f) Magnesium + Sulphuric Acid ⟶

g) ⟶ Iron Sulphate + Hydrogen

h) ⟶ Aluminium Oxide

3. Why would you not attempt to carry out the reaction between potassium and dilute hydrochloric acid?

4. a) Explain, using diagrams, why an iron nail becomes coated with copper when it is put into a solution of copper sulphate.

b) What would happen if a gold ring was put into a solution of copper sulphate. Explain your answer?

5. Complete the word equations for the following displacement reactions. If there is no reaction write 'no reaction'.

a) Tin + Copper Sulphate ⟶

b) Lead + Copper Sulphate ⟶

c) Silver + Copper Sulphate ⟶

d) Gold + Copper Sulphate ⟶

e) Magnesium + Lead Nitrate ⟶

f) Tin + Lead Nitrate ⟶

g) Carbon + Zinc Oxide ⟶

h) Carbon + Aluminium Oxide ⟶

i) Hydrogen + Zinc Oxide ⟶

j) Hydrogen + Copper Oxide ⟶

6. a) What is an ore?

b) What is reduction?

c) How are metals above carbon in the reactivity series extracted from their ores?

7. The diagram opposite shows a blast furnace used for the extraction of iron.
    a) Which THREE substances are fed into the top of the furnace?
    b) What passes into the furnace via the tuyeres?
    c) Apart from iron, what else is removed from the bottom of the furnace?
    d) Give THREE uses for iron.

8. a) Complete the following word equations which show the three reactions which
       occur inside the furnace.
       (i) Carbon   +   Oxygen ——————→
       (ii) Carbon Dioxide   +   Carbon ——————→
       (iii) Iron Oxide   +   Carbon Monoxide ——————→
    b) For each reaction above write a balanced symbol equation.
    c) What is oxidation? Explain your answer with reference to one of the equations above.

9. a) Explain why aluminium cannot be extracted from its ore using the same process
       as for iron.
    b) What is the name of the process used to extract aluminium?
    c) In the extraction process which other product is also formed?

10. What is a redox reaction? Explain your answer with reference to the reactions that occur at the electrodes
    during the electrolysis of aluminium.

11. Explain, using diagrams, how copper can be obtained in a pure form using electrolysis.

12. Why is rusting an example of an oxidation reaction?

13. a) Why is it important that zinc bars are attached to the hulls of ships?
    b) Some iron objects are galvanised using zinc. Explain how this prevents the iron from rusting even if the
       object is scratched.
    c) Why are knives and forks made from stainless steel?
    d) Why doesn't aluminium, which is higher than iron in the reactivity series, corrode away as quickly as you
       would expect?

14. The equation below shows the reaction that takes place in the production of ammonia.

    a) Name 'A' and 'B'.   A + B ⇌ Ammonia
    b) Ammonia is used to make ammonium nitrate, a fertiliser (i) which acid is reacted with ammonia to make
       ammonium nitrate? (ii) why is this an example of a neutralising reaction? (iii) what problems do nitrogen-
       based fertilisers cause if they find their way into our water system?

15. The amount or percentage of ammonia formed will change if the pressure and temperature is changed.
    a) Why is ammonia produced at a pressure of 200 atmospheres and a temperature of 450°C?
    b) What happens to the percentage of ammonia produced if this temperature is increased?
       Is this an advantage or a disadvantage?
    c) What happens to the percentage of ammonia produced if the pressure is increased?
       Is this an advantage or a disadvantage?

Using Chemical Symbols

• Each element is represented by a different symbol ...
  ... eg. Fe for iron, Na for sodium, C for carbon, and O for oxygen.
• These symbols are all contained in the PERIODIC TABLE (See P.76).
• These symbols can be used to represent molecules of compounds and can show us the RATIO OF ATOMS OF DIFFERENT ELEMENTS which are combined to form the compounds. These are chemical formulae eg. ...

$$H_2O \qquad\qquad CO_2 \qquad\qquad NH_3$$

Writing Formulae

• Before you can start writing formulae on your own it is important that you understand what formulae show.
• Chemists use formulae to show ...
• ... the different elements and ...
• ... the number of atoms of each element in a substance.

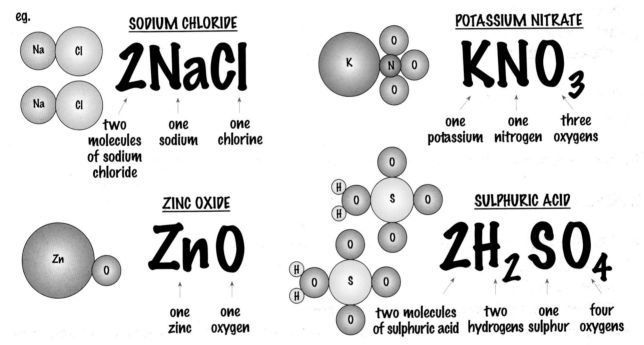

eg.

SODIUM CHLORIDE

$2NaCl$

two molecules of sodium chloride | one sodium | one chlorine

POTASSIUM NITRATE

KNO_3

one potassium | one nitrogen | three oxygens

ZINC OXIDE

ZnO

one zinc | one oxygen

SULPHURIC ACID

$2H_2SO_4$

two molecules of sulphuric acid | two hydrogens | one sulphur | four oxygens

If brackets are put around part of the formula remember to multiply everything inside the bracket by the number outside.

eg.

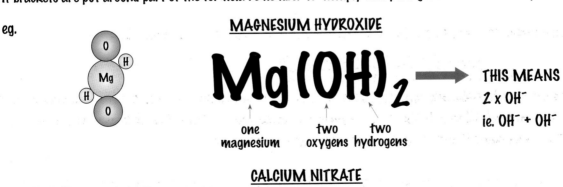

MAGNESIUM HYDROXIDE

$Mg(OH)_2$ → THIS MEANS $2 \times OH^-$ ie. $OH^- + OH^-$

one magnesium | two oxygens | two hydrogens

CALCIUM NITRATE

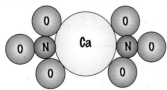

$Ca(NO_3)_2$ → THIS MEANS $2 \times NO_3^-$ ie. $NO_3^- + NO_3^-$

one calcium | two nitrogens | six oxygens

Writing Equations

You can show what has happened during a reaction using a WORD equation ...
... with the substances reacting ie. the REACTANTS, on one side of the equation ...
... and the new substances formed ie. the PRODUCTS, on the other.

$$REACTANTS \longrightarrow PRODUCTS$$

eg.   SODIUM   +   WATER $\longrightarrow$ SODIUM HYDROXIDE   +   HYDROGEN

Reactants   Products

This reaction can also be represented using a SYMBOL equation.

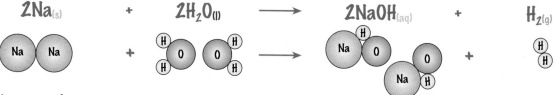

$$2Na_{(s)} \quad + \quad 2H_2O_{(l)} \quad \longrightarrow \quad 2NaOH_{(aq)} \quad + \quad H_{2(g)}$$

... This means that ...

| 2 atoms of sodium which is <u>solid</u> | and | 2 molecules of water which is <u>liquid</u> | produce | 2 molecules of sodium hydroxide in <u>aqueous</u> solution | and | 1 molecule of hydrogen which is a <u>gas</u> |

- (s), (l), (aq) and (g) are known as the STATE SYMBOLS.

Another example ...

HYDROGEN   +   OXYGEN $\longrightarrow$ WATER
$$2H_{2(g)} \quad + \quad O_{2(g)} \quad \longrightarrow \quad 2H_2O_{(l)}$$

What You Really Need To Know

For the tier of the syllabus for which you are entered, you need to be able to ...

- ... write WORD EQUATIONS for ALL reactions referred to in your tier.
- ... recall the FORMULAE of ALL SIMPLE COVALENT COMPOUNDS referred to in your tier.
- ... write down the correct FORMULAE for SIMPLE IONIC COMPOUNDS.
- ... interpret CHEMICAL FORMULAE or SYMBOLIC REPRESENTATIONS of molecules.
- ... interpret supplied SYMBOL EQUATIONS including STATE SYMBOLS.

SIMPLE COVALENT FORMULAE

Water H_2O	Oxygen O_2
Carbon dioxide CO_2	Nitrogen N_2
Ammonia NH_3	Sulphur dioxide SO_2
Hydrogen H_2	

SIMPLE IONIC FORMULAE

Sodium chloride NaCl	Sodium hydroxide NaOH
Calcium chloride $CaCl_2$	Potassium hydroxide KOH
Magnesium oxide MgO	Calcium hydroxide $Ca(OH)_2$
Hydrochloric acid HCl	Calcium carbonate $CaCO_3$
Sulphuric acid H_2SO_4	Aluminium oxide Al_2O_3
Nitric acid HNO_3	Iron oxide Fe_2O_3

Some Important Principles

- The TOTAL MASS of the PRODUCT(S) of a chemical reaction is ALWAYS ...
  ... EXACTLY EQUAL to the TOTAL MASS of the REACTANT(S).
  This is because the products of a chemical reaction are made up from exactly the same atoms as the reactants!!
- Symbol chemical equations must, therefore, always be balanced. In other words ...

> THERE MUST BE THE SAME NUMBER OF ATOMS OF EACH ELEMENT ON THE REACTANT SIDE OF THE EQUATION AS THERE IS ON THE PRODUCT SIDE OF THE EQUATION.

Writing Balanced Symbol Equations

There are FOUR IMPORTANT STEPS ...

STEP 1: WRITE A WORD EQUATION FOR THE CHEMICAL REACTION.
STEP 2: SUBSTITUTE IN FORMULAE FOR THE ELEMENTS OR COMPOUNDS INVOLVED.
STEP 3: BALANCE THE EQUATION BY ADDING NUMBERS IN FRONT OF THE REACTANTS AND/OR PRODUCTS.
STEP 4: WRITE DOWN A BALANCED SYMBOL EQUATION INCLUDING STATE SYMBOLS.

EXAMPLE 1 - The reaction between magnesium and oxygen.

STEP 1: MAGNESIUM + OXYGEN $\longrightarrow$ MAGNESIUM OXIDE
STEP 2: Mg + O_2 $\longrightarrow$ MgO
STEP 3: 'REACTANTS' $\longrightarrow$ 'PRODUCT'

Mg + O O $\longrightarrow$ Mg O

But now, there's only one O on the 'product side', so we must add another MgO ...

Mg + O O $\longrightarrow$ Mg O Mg O

But now, there's only one Mg on the 'reactant side', so we must add another Mg ...

Mg Mg + O O $\longrightarrow$ Mg O Mg O

There are two magnesium atoms and two oxygen atoms on each side - IT'S BALANCED!!

STEP 4: $2Mg_{(s)}$ + $O_{2(g)}$ $\longrightarrow$ $2MgO_{(s)}$

EXAMPLE 2 - The production of ammonia.

STEP 1: NITROGEN + HYDROGEN $\rightleftharpoons$ AMMONIA
STEP 2: N_2 + H_2 $\rightleftharpoons$ NH_3
STEP 3: 'REACTANTS' $\rightleftharpoons$ 'PRODUCT'

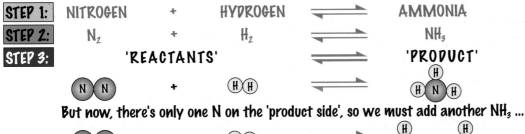

N N + H H $\rightleftharpoons$ H H N H

But now, there's only one N on the 'product side', so we must add another NH₃ ...

N N + H H $\rightleftharpoons$ H H N H H H N H

But now, there are only two H's on the 'reactant side', so we must add two more H₂'s ...

N N + H H H H H H $\rightleftharpoons$ H H N H H H N H

There are two nitrogen atoms and six hydrogen atoms on each side - IT'S BALANCED!!

STEP 4: $N_{2(g)}$ + $3H_{2(g)}$ $\rightleftharpoons$ $2NH_{3(g)}$

Relative Atomic Mass, A_r

Atoms are too small for their actual atomic mass to be of much use to us. To make things more manageable we use RELATIVE ATOMIC MASS, A_r. Basically this is just the MASS OF A PARTICULAR ATOM compared to the MASS OF AN ATOM OF HYDROGEN, (the lightest atom of all). In fact we now use $\frac{1}{12}$th the mass of a CARBON ATOM, but it doesn't make any real difference).

If we look at the periodic table we can see that all the elements have TWO NUMBERS.

Here are some common elements ...

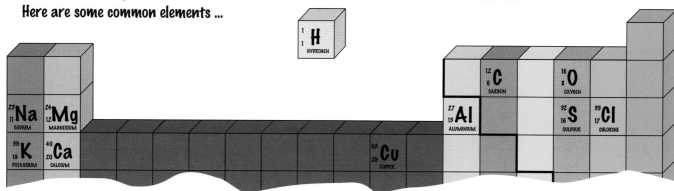

- The larger of the two numbers is the **MASS NUMBER** of the element but ...
  ... it also very conveniently doubles as the **RELATIVE ATOMIC MASS**, A_r of the element.
- So, in the examples above carbon is twelve times heavier than hydrogen, but ...
  ... is only half as heavy as magnesium, which is three quarters as heavy as sulphur ...
  ... which is twice as heavy as oxygen and so on, and so on ...
- We can use this idea to calculate the RELATIVE FORMULA MASS of compounds.

Relative Formula Mass, M_r

The relative formula mass of a compound is simply the relative atomic masses of all its elements added together. To calculate M_r, we need the FORMULA OF THE COMPOUND, and the A_r of ALL THE ATOMS INVOLVED.

EXAMPLE 1 - Using the data above, calculate the M_r of water, H_2O

STEP 1:	the formula ...	H_2O
STEP 2:	the A_r's ...	$(2 \times 1) + 16$
STEP 3:	the M_r ...	$2 + 16 = \underline{18}$

Since water has an M_r of 18, it is 18 times heavier than a hydrogen atom, or 1.5 times heavier than a carbon atom, or $\frac{2}{3}$ as heavy as an aluminium atom.

EXAMPLE 2 - Using the data above, calculate the M_r of sodium hydroxide, NaOH

STEP 1:	the formula ...	NaOH
STEP 2:	the A_r's ...	$23 + 16 + 1$
STEP 3:	the M_r ...	$23 + 16 + 1 = \underline{40}$

Since sodium hydroxide has an M_r of 40, it is as heavy as a calcium atom!

EXAMPLE 3 - Using the data above, calculate the M_r of potassium carbonate, K_2CO_3

STEP 1:	the formula ...	K_2CO_3
STEP 2:	the A_r's ...	$(39 \times 2) + 12 + (16 \times 3)$
STEP 3:	the M_r ...	$78 + 12 + 48 = \underline{\underline{138}}$

Calculating Percentages

If 12 pupils in a class of 30 are left-handed, you can work out the percentage of left-handers in the following way ...

$$\frac{\text{No. OF LEFT HANDERS}}{\text{TOTAL No. IN CLASS}} \times 100\% \quad \text{... in this case } \frac{12}{30} \times 100\% = \underline{40.0\%}$$

You use exactly the same principle in calculating percentage mass of an element in a compound, except this time we express it as ...

$$\frac{\text{MASS OF ELEMENT IN THE COMPOUND}}{\text{RELATIVE FORMULA MASS OF COMPOUND } (M_r)} \times 100\%$$

The mass of the compound is simply its relative formula mass and all you need to know is the FORMULA OF THE COMPOUND and the RELATIVE ATOMIC MASS of all the atoms.

Examples Of Percentage Mass Questions

EXAMPLE 1 - Calculate the percentage mass of magnesium in magnesium oxide, MgO.

MASS of magnesium = 24 (since this is its A_r, and there's only one atom of it!).

RELATIVE FORMULA MASS (M_r) of MgO = (A_r for Mg) 24 + (A_r for O) 16 = 40.

Substituting into our formula ... $\dfrac{\text{MASS OF ELEMENT}}{M_r \text{ OF COMPOUND}} \times 100\%$ ... we get $\frac{24}{40} \times 100\% = 60.0\%$

EXAMPLE 2 - Calculate the percentage mass of oxygen in calcium carbonate, $CaCO_3$.

MASS of oxygen = 16 x 3 = 48 (since its A_r is 16 and there are three atoms of it!).

RELATIVE FORMULA MASS (M_r) of $CaCO_3$ = (A_r for Ca) 40 + (A_r for C) 12 + (A_r for O x 3) 48 = 100.

Substituting into our formula ... $\dfrac{\text{MASS OF ELEMENT}}{M_r \text{ OF COMPOUND}} \times 100\%$ ... we get $\frac{48}{100} \times 100\% = 48.0\%$

EXAMPLE 3 - Calculate the percentage mass of potassium in potassium carbonate, K_2CO_3.

MASS of potassium = 39 x 2 = 78 (since its A_r is 39 and there are two atoms of it!).

RELATIVE FORMULA MASS (M_r) of K_2CO_3 = (A_r for K x 2) 78 + (A_r for C) 12 + (A_r for O x 3) 48 = 138.

Substituting into our formula ... $\dfrac{\text{MASS OF ELEMENT}}{M_r \text{ OF COMPOUND}} \times 100\%$ ... we get $\frac{78}{138} \times 100\% = 56.5\%$

In Summary ...

All we're really doing is DIVIDING THE MASS OF THE ELEMENT ...

... by the MASS OF THE COMPOUND and multiplying by 100!

● Just make sure you account for <u>all</u> the atoms in the element or compound.

We sometimes need to be able to work out how much of a substance is USED UP or PRODUCED in a chemical reaction, when we are given certain data. To do this we need to know ...
- ... the RELATIVE FORMULA MASS, M_r of the REACTANTS and PRODUCTS (or the A_r of all the elements).
- ... the BALANCED SYMBOL EQUATION for the reaction concerned.

By substituting the first of these into the second we can work out ...

THE RATIO OF MASS OF REACTANT TO MASS OF PRODUCT

... and then apply this ratio to the question.

Calculating The Mass Of A Product

EXAMPLE - Calculate how much calcium oxide can be produced from 50kg of calcium carbonate.
(Relative Atomic Masses: Ca = 40, C = 12, O = 16)

STEP 1: Write down the equation.

$$CaCO_{3(s)} \xrightarrow{HEAT} CaO_{(s)} + CO_{2(g)}$$

STEP 2: Work out the M_r of each substance.

$$40 + 12 + (3 \times 16) \longrightarrow (40 + 16) + [12 + (2 \times 16)]$$

STEP 3: CHECK the total mass of reactants = the total mass of the products. If they are not the same, check your work.

$$100 \longrightarrow 56 + 44 \checkmark$$

Since the question only mentions calcium oxide and calcium carbonate, you can now ignore the carbon dioxide!

This gives us ... THE RATIO OF MASS OF REACTANT ... $100 \longrightarrow 56$ ... TO MASS OF PRODUCT

STEP 4: Apply this ratio to the question ...

... if 100kg of $CaCO_3$ produces 56kg of CaO ...

... then 1kg of $CaCO_3$ produces $\frac{56}{100}$ kg of CaO ...

... and 50kg of $CaCO_3$ produces $\frac{56}{100} \times 50 = \underline{28kg\ of\ CaO}$.

Calculating The Mass Of A Reactant

EXAMPLE - Calculate how much aluminium oxide is needed to produce 540 tonnes of aluminium.
(Relative Atomic Masses: Al = 27, O = 16).

STEP 1: Write down the equation.

$$2Al_2O_{3(l)} \longrightarrow 4Al_{(l)} + 3O_{2(g)}$$

STEP 2: Work out the M_r of each substance.

$$2[(2 \times 27) + (3 \times 16)] \longrightarrow (4 \times 27) + [3 \times (2 \times 16)]$$

STEP 3: CHECK the total mass of reactants = the total mass of the products

$$204 \longrightarrow 108 + 96 \checkmark$$

Since the question only mentions aluminium oxide and aluminium, you can now ignore the oxygen!

This gives us ... THE RATIO OF MASS OF REACTANT ... $204 \longrightarrow 108$ ... TO MASS OF PRODUCT

STEP 4: Apply this ratio to the question ...

... if 204 tonnes of Al_2O_3 produces 108 tonnes of Al ...

... then $\frac{204}{108}$ tonnes is needed to produce 1 tonne of Al ...

... and $\frac{204}{108} \times 540$ tonnes is needed to produce 540 tonnes of Al.

ie. <u>1020 tonnes of Al_2O_3 is needed</u>

Firstly the mass of gas is calculated in exactly the same way as on the previous page.

Then, the mass of the gas must be converted into a volume, using this fact ...

THE RELATIVE FORMULA MASS (M_r) OF A GAS IN GRAMS OCCUPIES A VOLUME OF 24 LITRES ($24,000cm^3$) AT ORDINARY PRESSURE AND TEMPERATURE.

(Sometimes the conditions are referred to as atmospheric pressure and room temperature).

In other words 2 grams of hydrogen (H_2), 32 grams of oxygen (O_2) and 44 grams of carbon dioxide (CO_2) all occupy a volume of 24 litres at ordinary pressure and temperature.

Calculating The Volume Of A Product

EXAMPLE - Determine the volume of ammonia produced when 56g of nitrogen reacts completely with hydrogen (Relative Atomic Masses: N = 14, H = 1)

STEP 1: Write down the equation. $N_2 + 3H_2 \longrightarrow 2NH_3$

STEP 2: Work out the M_r of each substance. $(2 \times 14) + 3 \times (2 \times 1) \longrightarrow 2[14 + (3 \times 1)]$

STEP 3: Check the total mass of reactants $28 + 6 \longrightarrow 34$ ✓
= Total mass of products.

Since the question only applies to ammonia and nitrogen, you can now ignore the hydrogen!

This gives us ... THE RATIO OF MASS OF REACTANT ... $28 \longrightarrow 34$ ... TO MASS OF PRODUCT

STEP 4: Apply the ratios to the question ...   ... if 28g of nitrogen produces 34g of ammonia ...

... then 1g of nitrogen would produce $\frac{34}{28}$ g of ammonia ...

... and 56g of nitrogen would produce $\frac{34}{28} \times 56 = 68g$ of ammonia

STEP 5: Convert this mass to a volume ... M_r OF A GAS IN GRAMS OCCUPIES 24 LITRES

17g of ammonia would occupy 24 litres ...

... and so 1g of ammonia would occupy $\frac{24}{17}$ litres ...

... and 68g of ammonia would occupy $\frac{24}{17} \times 68 = \underline{96\ litres}$

Calculating The Volume Of A Reactant

EXAMPLE - Determine the volume of methane burnt completely in oxygen if 11g of carbon dioxide is produced. (Relative Atomic Masses: C = 12, O = 16, H = 1).

STEP 1: Write down the equation. $CH_4 + 2O_2 \longrightarrow CO_2 + 2H_2O$

STEP 2: Work out the M_r of each substance. $12 + (4 \times 1) + 2 \times (2 \times 16) \longrightarrow 12 + (2 \times 16) + 2[(2 \times 1) + 16]$

STEP 3: Check the total mass of reactants $16 + 64 \longrightarrow 44 + 36$ ✓
= Total mass of products.

Since the question only applies to carbon dioxide and methane, you can now ignore the oxygen and water!

This gives us ... THE RATIO OF MASS OF REACTANT ... $16 \longrightarrow 44$ ... TO MASS OF PRODUCT

STEP 4: Apply the ratios to the question ...   ... if 16g of methane produces 44g of carbon dioxide ...

... then $\frac{16}{44}$ g of methane is needed to produce 1g of CO_2 ...

... and $\frac{16}{44} \times 11 = 4g$ of methane is needed to produce 11g of CO_2

STEP 5: Convert this mass to a volume ... M_r OF A GAS IN GRAMS OCCUPIES 24 LITRES

16g of CH_4 would occupy 24 litres ...

... and so 1g of CH_4 would occupy $\frac{24}{16}$ litres ...

... and 4g of CH_4 would occupy $\frac{24}{16} \times 4 = \underline{6\ litres}$ ...

EMPIRICAL FORMULAE

HIGHER TIER

The empirical formula is the simplest formula which represents the RATIO OF ATOMS IN A COMPOUND. There's one simple rule ...

ALWAYS DIVIDE THE DATA YOU ARE GIVEN BY THE A_r OF THE ELEMENT.

You then simplify the ratio to give you the simplest formula.

EXAMPLE 1

Find the simplest formula of an oxide of iron, formed by reacting 2.24g of iron with 0.96g of oxygen. (Relative Atomic Masses: Fe = 56, O = 16).

STEP 1: Divide masses by A_r — For iron $\frac{2.24}{56}$ For oxygen $\frac{0.96}{16}$

STEP 2: Write down the ratio — 0.04 : 0.06

STEP 3: Simplify this ratio — 2 : 3

STEP 4: Write formula — simplest formula is Fe_2O_3

EXAMPLE 2

Find the simplest formula of an oxide of magnesium which contains 60% magnesium and 40% oxygen by weight (Relative Atomic Masses: Mg = 24, O = 16).

Just treat the percentages as if they were grams ...

STEP 1: Divide masses by A_r — For magnesium $\frac{60}{24}$ For oxygen $\frac{40}{16}$

STEP 2: Write down the ratio — 2.5 : 2.5

STEP 3: Simplify this ratio — 1 : 1

STEP 4: Write formula — simplest formula is MgO

EXAMPLE 3

Find the simplest formula of a compound which contains 10g of calcium, 3g of carbon and 12g of oxygen. (Relative Atomic Masses: Ca = 40, C = 12, O = 16).

STEP 1: Divide masses by A_r — For calcium $\frac{10}{40}$ For carbon $\frac{3}{12}$ For oxygen $\frac{12}{16}$

STEP 2: Write down the ratio — 0.25 : 0.25 : 0.75

STEP 3: Simplify this ratio — 1 : 1 : 3

STEP 4: Write formula — simplest formula is $CaCO_3$

EXAMPLE 4

Find the simplest formula of a compound which contains 1.2g of magnesium, 1.6g of oxygen and 0.1g of hydrogen. (Relative Atomic Masses: Mg = 24, O = 16, H = 1).

STEP 1: Divide masses by A_r — For magnesium $\frac{1.2}{24}$ For oxygen $\frac{1.6}{16}$ For hydrogen $\frac{0.1}{1}$

STEP 2: Write down the ratio — 0.05 : 0.1 : 0.1

STEP 3: Simplify this ratio — 1 : 2 : 2

STEP 4: Write formula — simplest formula is $Mg(OH)_2$ and NOT MgO_2H_2 !!

Electrolysis is the breaking down of a compound containing IONS (charged particles) into its ELEMENTS by using an ELECTRIC CURRENT.

Balancing Half-equations

During electrolysis ions gain or lose electrons at the electrodes ...
... forming ELECTRICALLY NEUTRAL ATOMS or MOLECULES which are then released. (ie. they have no charge).
If we consider the electrolysis of COPPER CHLORIDE SOLUTION ...

At the POSITIVE ELECTRODE chloride IONS give up an electron and form chlorine MOLECULES

$$Cl^- - e^- \longrightarrow Cl_2$$

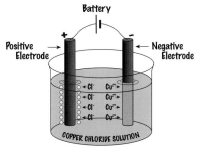

At the NEGATIVE ELECTRODE copper IONS pick up TWO electrons and become copper ATOMS.

$$Cu^{2+} + 2e^- \longrightarrow Cu$$

The reactions occurring at the electrodes are called HALF-EQUATIONS, but the one at the positive electrode clearly needs balancing since there is only one Cl on the left-hand side and two on the right.

$$2Cl^- - 2e^- \longrightarrow Cl_2$$

(NB) You will need to be able to complete and balance supplied half-equations!

Calculation Of Mass/Volume Of The Products Of Electrolysis

EXAMPLE
If 2g of copper is deposited at the negative electrode during the electrolysis of copper chloride, calculate the volume of chlorine released.

STEP 1: Write down the half-equations occurring at the electrodes.
NEGATIVE ELECTRODE: $Cu^{2+} + 2e^- \longrightarrow Cu_{(s)}$
POSITIVE ELECTRODE: $2Cl^- - 2e^- \longrightarrow Cl_{2(g)}$ (chlorine exists as molecules remember.)

As you can see, the same amount of charge ($2e^-$) liberates 1 atom of copper and 1 molecule of chlorine.
But since the A_r of Cu is 63 and the A_r of Cl is 35, this means that ...
... 63g of copper and 70g (2 x 35) of chlorine (the M_r) are liberated by the same amount of charge.
These two figures (63g and 70g) represent the relative masses liberated by the same charge. In other words, when 63g of copper is deposited then 70g of chlorine is also liberated.

This gives us ... THE RATIO OF COPPER DEPOSITED ... 63 : 70 ... TO RATIO OF CHLORINE LIBERATED

STEP 2: Apply this ratio to the question ... ... if 63g of deposited copper liberates 70g of chlorine ...
... then 1g of deposited copper liberates $\frac{70}{63}$ g of chlorine ...
... and 2g of deposited copper liberates $\frac{70}{63}$ x 2g = 2.22g of chlorine.

STEP 3: Convert this mass to a volume ... M_r OF A GAS IN GRAMS OCCUPIES 24 LITRES.
70g of chlorine would occupy 24 litres ...
... and so 1g of chlorine would occupy $\frac{24}{70}$ litres ...
... and 2.22g of chlorine would occupy $\frac{24}{70}$ x 2.22g = 0.76 litres or 760cm³

* IMPORTANT POINT!
In cases where the same charge doesn't liberate the same amounts eg. ...
... $2H^+(aq) + 2e^- = H_2(g)$ and $O^{2-}(aq) - 2e^- = O(g)$, use the exact relative mass
ie. in this case, H_2 would be 2, and O would be 16 (not 32!)

ATOMS, ELEMENTS, COMPOUNDS AND CHEMICAL REACTIONS

WRITING FORMULAE

CALCIUM NITRATE

$$Ca(NO_3)_2$$

one calcium · two nitrogens · six oxygens

THIS MEANS
$2 \times NO_3^-$
ie. $NO_3^- + NO_3^-$

WRITING EQUATIONS   REACTANTS ⟶ PRODUCTS

Word equations can be used ...

eg. SODIUM + WATER ⟶ SODIUM HYDROXIDE + HYDROGEN

• Symbol equations can also be used ...

Na + H_2O ⟶ $NaOH$ + H_2

However, this isn't balanced (see next page).

• A balanced symbol equation can be used ...

$2Na$ + $2H_2O$ ⟶ $2NaOH$ + H_2

• ... with state symbols ...

$2Na_{(s)}$ + $2H_2O_{(l)}$ ⟶ $2NaOH_{(aq)}$ + $H_2{}_{(g)}$

SIMPLE COVALENT AND IONIC FORMULAE

SIMPLE COVALENT FORMULAE	
Water H_2O	Oxygen O_2
Carbon dioxide CO_2	Nitrogen N_2
Ammonia NH_3	Sulphur dioxide SO_2
Hydrogen H_2	

SIMPLE IONIC FORMULAE	
Sodium chloride $NaCl$	Sodium hydroxide $NaOH$
Calcium chloride $CaCl_2$	Potassium hydroxide KOH
Magnesium oxide MgO	Calcium hydroxide $Ca(OH)_2$
Hydrochloric acid HCl	Calcium carbonate $CaCO_3$
Sulphuric acid H_2SO_4	Aluminium oxide Al_2O_3
Nitric acid HNO_3	Iron oxide Fe_2O_3

WRITING BALANCED CHEMICAL EQUATIONS

'There must be the same number of atoms of each element on the reactant side of the equation as there is on the product side'.

STEP 1: WRITE A WORD EQUATION FOR THE CHEMICAL REACTION.

STEP 2: SUBSTITUTE IN FORMULAE FOR THE ELEMENTS OR COMPOUNDS INVOLVED.

STEP 3: BALANCE THE EQUATION BY ADDING NUMBERS IN FRONT OF THE REACTANTS AND/OR PRODUCTS.

STEP 4: WRITE DOWN A BALANCED SYMBOL EQUATION INCLUDING STATE SYMBOLS.

Example ...

STEP 1: MAGNESIUM + OXYGEN ⟶ MAGNESIUM OXIDE

STEP 2: Mg + O_2 ⟶ MgO

STEP 3: 'REACTANTS' ⟶ 'PRODUCT'

But now, there's only one O on the 'product side', so we must add another MgO ...

But now, there's only one Mg on the 'reactant side', so we must add another Mg ...

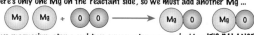

There are two magnesium atoms and two oxygen atoms on each side - IT'S BALANCED!!

STEP 4: $2Mg_{(s)}$ + $O_2{}_{(g)}$ ⟶ $2MgO_{(s)}$

RELATIVE ATOMIC MASS AND FORMULA MASS

RELATIVE ATOMIC MASS, A_r

The relative atomic mass, A_r is the mass of a particular atom of an element compared to the mass of an atom of hydrogen.

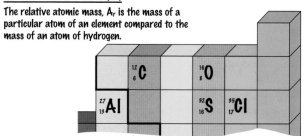

• The MASS NUMBER of an element also conveniently doubles as the RELATIVE ATOMIC MASS, A_r of the element.

RELATIVE FORMULA MASS, M_r

The relative formula mass, M_r of a compound is simply the relative atomic masses of all its elements added together.

Example ... Find the M_r of water, H_2O.

STEP 1: the formula ... H_2O

STEP 2: the A_r's ... $(2 \times 1) + 16$

STEP 3: the M_r ... $2 + 16 = \underline{18}$

PERCENTAGE MASS AND EMPIRICAL FORMULAE

CALCULATING % MASS OF AN ELEMENT IN A COMPOUND

$$\frac{\text{MASS OF ELEMENT IN THE COMPOUND}}{\text{RELATIVE FORMULA MASS OF COMPOUND } (M_r)} \times 100\%$$

Example ...
Calculate the % mass of magnesium in magnesium oxide.

MASS OF MAGNESIUM = 24 (since this is its A_r, and there's only one atom of it!).

RELATIVE FORMULA MASS (M_r) of MgO = (A_r for Mg) 24 + (A_r for O) 16 = 40.

Substituting into our formula ...

$$\frac{\text{MASS OF ELEMENT}}{M_r \text{ OF COMPOUND}} \times 100\% \text{, ... we get } \frac{24}{40} \times 100 = 60.0\%$$

EMPIRICAL FORMULAE This is the simplest formula which represents the RATIO OF ATOMS IN A COMPOUND. One simple rule ...

ALWAYS DIVIDE THE DATA YOU ARE GIVEN BY THE A_r OF THE ELEMENT.

Example ...
Find the simplest formula of an oxide of iron, formed by reacting 2.24g of iron with 0.96g of oxygen. (Relative Atomic Masses: Fe = 56, O = 16).

STEP 1: Divide masses by A_r For iron $\frac{2.24}{56}$ For oxygen $\frac{0.96}{16}$

STEP 2: Write down the ratio   0.04 : 0.06

STEP 3: Simplify this ratio   2 : 3

STEP 4: Write formula   Simplest Formula is Fe_2O_3

CALCULATING MASSES/VOLUMES OF PRODUCTS AND REACTANTS

BASIC PRINCIPLES you will need to know ...

• the RELATIVE FORMULA MASS, M_r of the reactants and products (or the A_r of all the elements).

• the BALANCED SYMBOL EQUATION for the reaction concerned.

You can then work out ...

• the RATIO OF MASS OF REACTANT TO MASS OF PRODUCT and then apply it to the question.

If you are calculating the volume of a gas you need to use this fact ...

• THE RELATIVE FORMULA MASS (M_r) OF A GAS IN GRAMS OCCUPIES A VOLUME OF 24 LITRES (24,000cm³) AT ORDINARY PRESSURE AND TEMPERATURE.

Example ... Determine the mass and volume of ammonia produced when 56g of nitrogen reacts completely with hydrogen.

STEP 1: Write down the equation. $N_2 + 3H_2 \longrightarrow 2NH_3$

STEP 2: Work out the M_r of each substance. $(2 \times 14) + 3 \times (2 \times 1) \longrightarrow 2[14 + (3 \times 1)]$

STEP 3: Check the total mass of reactants = Total mass of products. $28 + 6 \longrightarrow 34 \checkmark$

STEP 4: Apply the ratios to the question ...   ... If 28g of nitrogen produces 34g of ammonia ...

... then 1g of nitrogen would produce $\frac{34}{28}$ g of ammonia ...

... and 56g of nitrogen would produce $\frac{34}{28} \times 56 = 68g$ of ammonia

If you are asked to calculate mass, you stop at this point. However to calculate volume as well, there is one more step.

STEP 5: Convert this mass to a volume ... M_r OF A GAS IN GRAMS OCCUPIES 24 LITRES

17g of ammonia would occupy 24 litres ...

... and so 1g of ammonia would occupy $\frac{24}{17}$ litres ...

... and 68g of ammonia would occupy $\frac{24}{17} \times 68g = 96$ litres

ELECTROLYSIS CALCULATIONS

ELECTROLYSIS

Electrolysis is the breaking down of a compound containing IONS into its ELEMENTS by using an electric current.

Example ... If 2g of copper is deposited at the negative electrode during the electrolysis of copper chloride, calculate the volume of chlorine released.

STEP 1 Write down the half-equations occurring at the electrode.

+ve ELECTRODE	-ve ELECTRODE
$2Cl^- - 2e^- \longrightarrow Cl_2{}_{(g)}$	$Cu^{2+} + 2e^- \longrightarrow Cu_{(s)}$
(chlorine exists as molecules)	

The same amount of charge ($2e^-$) liberates 1 atom of copper and 1 molecule of chlorine. But since the A_r of Cu is 63 and the A_r of Cl is 35, this means that 63g of copper and 70g (2×35) of chlorine (the M_r) are liberated by the same amount of charge. ie. when 63g of copper is deposited then 70g of chlorine is also liberated.

This gives us ... THE RATIO OF COPPER DEPOSITED ... 63 : 70 ... TO RATIO OF CHLORINE LIBERATED

STEP 2: Apply this ratio to the question ...   ... if 63g of deposited copper liberates 70g of chlorine ...

... then 1g of deposited copper liberates $\frac{70}{63}$ of chlorine ...

... and 2g of deposited copper liberates $\frac{70}{63} \times 2g = 2.22g$ of chlorine.

STEP 3: Convert this mass to a volume ... M_r OF A GAS IN GRAMS OCCUPIES 24 LITRES.

70g of chlorine would occupy 24 litres ...

... and so 1g of chlorine would occupy $\frac{24}{70}$ litres ...

... and 2.22g of chlorine would occupy $\frac{24}{70} \times 2.22g = 0.76$ litre or 760cm³

Please refer to the periodic table for A_r of substances involved.

1. In terms of elements present, and numbers of atoms involved, what do the following formulae represent?

    $Ca(OH)_2$ KNO_3 Na_2CO_3

2. Explain what the state symbols are and give an example of an equation with them in.

3. Write down the formulae for the following simple ionic compounds ...
   sodium chloride, magnesium oxide, sulphuric acid, sodium hydroxide and calcium carbonate.

4. Write balanced symbol equations for the following reactions:
   a) Potassium   +   Water $\longrightarrow$ Potassium Hydroxide   +   Hydrogen
   b) Sodium Hydroxide   +   Sulphuric Acid $\longrightarrow$ Potassium Sulphate   +   Water
   c) Hydrogen   +   Chlorine $\longrightarrow$ Hydrogen Chloride
   d) Calcium   +   Water $\longrightarrow$ Calcium Hydroxide   +   Hydrogen
   e) Iron   +   Oxygen $\longrightarrow$ Iron Oxide

5. Calculate the relative formula mass of the following compounds:

Water, H_2O	Ammonia, NH_3
Carbon Dioxide, CO_2	Sodium Chloride, $NaCl$
Methane, CH_4	Sodium Carbonate, Na_2CO_3
Nitrogen, N_2	Ammonium Chloride, NH_4Cl

6. What is the essential difference between relative atomic mass and relative formula mass?

7. Calculate the relative formula masses of all the compounds in the following symbol equation ...

    $NaOH$ + HCl $\longrightarrow$ $NaCl$ + H_2O

8. Calculate the percentage mass of oxygen in water, H_2O.

9. Calculate the percentage mass of oxygen in carbon dioxide, CO_2.

10. Calculate the percentage mass of carbon in methane, CH_4.

11. Calculate the percentage mass of nitrogen in ammonia, NH_3.

12. Calculate the percentage mass of chlorine in sodium chloride, $NaCl$.

13. Calculate the percentage mass of oxygen in sodium carbonate, Na_2CO_3.

14. Calculate the percentage mass of hydrogen in ammonium chloride, NH_4Cl.

15. What mass of aluminium is produced by the electrolysis of 38.5 tonnes of aluminium oxide?

    $2Al_2O_{3(s)}$ $\longrightarrow$ $4Al_{(s)}$ + $3O_{2(g)}$

16. What mass of calcium oxide is produced by the thermal decomposition of 27 tonnes of calcium carbonate?

    $CaCO_{3(s)}$ $\longrightarrow$ $CaO_{(s)}$ + $CO_{2(g)}$

17. What mass of hydrogen chloride gas is produced by the thermal decomposition of 6.0g of ammonium chloride?

$$NH_4Cl_{(s)} \longrightarrow NH_{3(g)} + HCl_{(g)}$$

18. What mass of copper is produced from the electrolysis of 87g of copper chloride?

$$CuCl_{2(aq)} \longrightarrow Cu_{(s)} + Cl_{2(g)}$$

19. What mass of calcium carbonate would need to be decomposed to produce 27 kilograms of calcium oxide?

$$CaCO_{3(s)} \longrightarrow CaO_{(s)} + CO_{2(g)}$$

20. Find the volume of ammonia formed when 7.5g of ammonium chloride is heated.

$$NH_4Cl_{(s)} \longrightarrow NH_{3(g)} + HCl_{(g)}$$

21. Find the simplest formula of a chloride of sodium formed by reacting 4.6g of sodium with 7.0g of chlorine (A_r: Na = 23, Cl = 35).

22. Find the simplest formula of an oxide of carbon formed by reacting 1.2g of carbon with 3.2g of oxygen (A_r: C = 12, O = 16).

23. a) What is electrolysis?

   b) The diagram below shows the electrolysis of copper chloride. Write down balanced half-equations for the reactions occurring at the two electrodes.

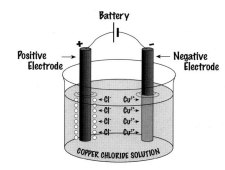

24. Balance the following half-equation: $O^{2-} - 2e^- \longrightarrow O_2$

25. If 2.3g of copper is deposited at the negative electrode during electrolysis of copper chloride, calculate the mass and volume of chlorine released.

26. If 0.5 litres of chlorine gas is released during the electrolysis of copper chloride, calculate the mass of copper deposited at the negative electrode.

27. During the electrolysis of molten lead bromide, lead is deposited at the negative electrode and bromine gas is produced at the positive electrode.
   a) Write balanced half-equations for the reactions occurring at the two electrodes.
   b) If 3g of lead is deposited at the negative electrode during the electrolysis, calculate the mass and volume of bromine released.

The Periodic Table

The chemical elements can be arranged in order of their RELATIVE ATOMIC MASSES. The list can then be arranged in rows so that elements with similar properties are in the same columns, or GROUPS.
This forms the basis of the PERIODIC TABLE ...

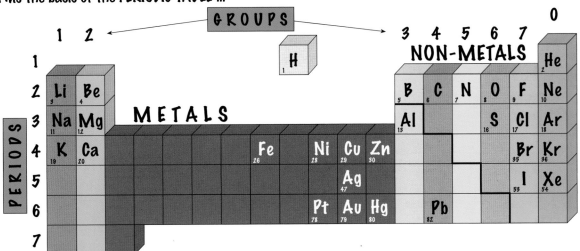

In the modern periodic table, the elements are arranged in order of atomic number since arranging them in order of relative atomic mass results in some oddities such as argon ending up in Group 1 while potassium goes to Group 0!! (instead of the other way round!).

Key Points About The Periodic Table

The periodic table can be seen to be an arrangement of the elements in terms of their electronic structure ...
- ELEMENTS in the SAME GROUP have the SAME NUMBER OF ELECTRONS IN THEIR OUTERMOST SHELL. This number also coincides with the GROUP NUMBER. Elements in the same group have SIMILAR PROPERTIES.
- From left to right, ACROSS EACH PERIOD A PARTICULAR ENERGY LEVEL IS GRADUALLY FILLED WITH ELECTRONS. In the next period, the next energy level is filled etc. (see P.8 for electronic structure).
- More than ³/₄ of the elements are METALS. They are found mainly in Groups 1 and 2 and in the central block.
- The rest are obviously NON-METALS. They are found in the Groups at the right-hand side of the periodic table.

Early Attempts To Classify The Elements

JOHN NEWLANDS (1864)

Newlands only knew of the existence of 63 elements. Many were undiscovered. He arranged the known elements in order of RELATIVE ATOMIC MASS and found similarities amongst every eighth element in the series.

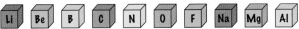

This makes sense since the NOBLE GASES (Group 0) weren't discovered until 1894. In other words he noticed PERIODICITY although the 'missing' elements caused problems.

DIMITRI MENDELEEV (1869)

Mendeleev realised that some elements had yet to be discovered, so he left gaps to accommodate their eventual discovery.

He used his periodic table to PREDICT THE EXISTENCE OF OTHER ELEMENTS.

MODERN CHEMISTRY

Although scientists used to regard the periodic table as a curiosity, then as a useful tool, the discovery of ELECTRONIC STRUCTURE gives us a more sound base for the table since the key to similarities amongst elements is the NUMBER OF ELECTRONS IN THE OUTERMOST ENERGY LEVEL ie. Group 1 elements have 1 electron in their outermost energy level, Group 2 elements have 2 electrons and so on.

Group 1 – The Alkali Metals

- The alkali metals all have a low density, ...
  ... the first three being less dense than water, consequently they float.
- Their melting and boiling points decrease as we go down the group.

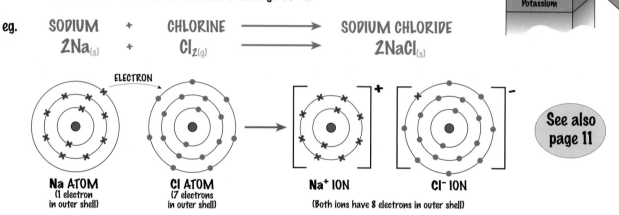

GROUP 1

Li Lithium

Na Sodium

K Potassium

MORE REACTIVE

LOWER MELTING & BOILING POINTS

Reaction Of Alkali Metals With Non-metals

Alkali metals react with non-metals to produce IONIC COMPOUNDS.
The metal atom LOSES ONE ELECTRON ...
... to form a METAL ION which carries a charge of +1.

eg.
$$\text{SODIUM} + \text{CHLORINE} \longrightarrow \text{SODIUM CHLORIDE}$$
$$2Na_{(s)} + Cl_{2(g)} \longrightarrow 2NaCl_{(s)}$$

ELECTRON

Na ATOM
(1 electron in outer shell)

Cl ATOM
(7 electrons in outer shell)

Na⁺ ION

Cl⁻ ION

(Both ions have 8 electrons in outer shell)

See also page 11

The ionic compounds formed are WHITE SOLIDS which dissolve in water to form COLOURLESS SOLUTIONS.

Reaction Of Alkali Metals With Water

Alkali metals react with water to produce HYDROXIDES, which dissolve in water to form alkaline solutions, and HYDROGEN.

eg.
$$\text{POTASSIUM} + \text{WATER} \longrightarrow \text{POTASSIUM HYDROXIDE} + \text{HYDROGEN}$$
$$2K_{(s)} + 2H_2O_{(l)} \longrightarrow 2KOH_{(aq)} + H_{2(g)}$$

As we go down the group the alkali metals become MORE REACTIVE and so they react more VIGOROUSLY with water. They float, may melt and the hydrogen gas produced may ignite!! Lithium reacts gently, sodium more aggressively and potassium so aggressively it melts and catches fire.

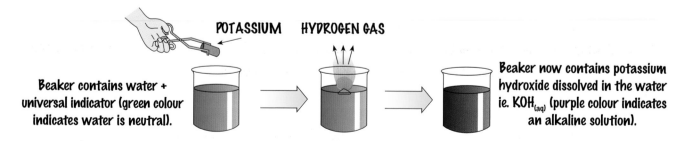

POTASSIUM   HYDROGEN GAS

Beaker contains water + universal indicator (green colour indicates water is neutral).

Beaker now contains potassium hydroxide dissolved in the water ie. KOH$_{(aq)}$ (purple colour indicates an alkaline solution).

A simple laboratory test for the hydrogen gas produced ...
... is that when a test tube of hydrogen is held to a flame ...
... the hydrogen burns with a squeaky explosion (POP!)

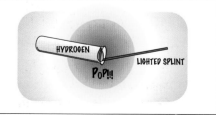

HYDROGEN

LIGHTED SPLINT

POP!!!

Group 7 - The Halogens

There are five non-metals in this group.

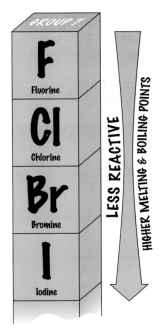

- The halogens have low melting and boiling points, ...
  ... which increase as we go down the group.
- At room temperature fluorine and chlorine are gases ...
  ... and bromine is a liquid.
- They all have coloured vapours, which in the case of chlorine and bromine
  are extremely pungent.
- They exist as **MOLECULES** made up of pairs of atoms.

   ... bromine molecules

- They are **BRITTLE** and **CRUMBLY** when **SOLID** ...
- ... and **POOR CONDUCTORS** of **HEAT** and **ELECTRICITY** even when solid or liquid.
- As we go down the group the halogens become **LESS REACTIVE**.

Reaction Of Halogens With Metals

Halogens react with metals to produce **IONIC SALTS**.
The halogen atom **GAINS ONE ELECTRON** to form a **HALIDE ION** which carries a charge of -1.

eg.   LITHIUM   +   CHLORINE $\longrightarrow$ LITHIUM CHLORIDE
       $2Li_{(s)}$ + $Cl_{2(g)}$ $\longrightarrow$ $2LiCl_{(s)}$

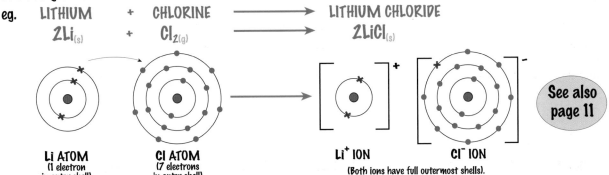

Li ATOM (1 electron in outer shell)   Cl ATOM (7 electrons in outer shell) Li^+ ION Cl^- ION
(Both ions have full outermost shells).

See also page 11

Reaction Of Halogens With Other Non-metallic Elements

Halogens react with other non-metallic elements to form **MOLECULAR COMPOUNDS**.

eg.   HYDROGEN   +   CHLORINE $\longrightarrow$ HYDROGEN CHLORIDE
       $H_{2(g)}$ + $Cl_{2(g)}$ $\longrightarrow$ $2HCl_{(g)}$

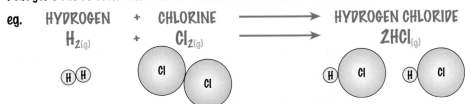

Displacement Reactions Of Halogens

A MORE REACTIVE HALOGEN will **DISPLACE** a **LESS REACTIVE HALOGEN** from an aqueous solution of its salt
ie. chlorine will displace both bromine and iodine while bromine will displace iodine.

eg.   POTASSIUM IODIDE   +   CHLORINE $\longrightarrow$ POTASSIUM CHLORIDE   +   IODINE
       $2KI_{(aq)}$ + $Cl_{2(g)}$ $\longrightarrow$ $2KCl_{(aq)}$ + $I_{2(aq)}$

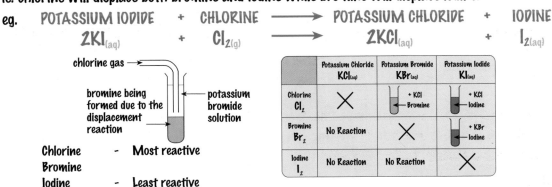

chlorine gas →
bromine being formed due to the displacement reaction
potassium bromide solution

Chlorine   -   Most reactive
Bromine
Iodine   -   Least reactive

	Potassium Chloride $KCl_{(aq)}$	Potassium Bromide $KBr_{(aq)}$	Potassium Iodide $KI_{(aq)}$
Chlorine Cl_2	✕	+ KCl ← Bromine	+ KCl ← Iodine
Bromine Br_2	No Reaction	✕	+ KBr ← Iodine
Iodine I_2	No Reaction	No Reaction	✕

Group 0 – The Noble Gases

There are SIX GASES in this group.

- The noble gases all have low melting and boiling points.
- At room temperature they are all gases.
- They are brittle and crumbly when solid.
- They are poor conductors of heat and electricity (even when solid or liquid).
- They exist as INDIVIDUAL ATOMS (monatomic).
  eg. He, Ne, Ar etc. rather than in pairs (diatomic) like other gaseous elements (Cl_2, H_2 etc.)

     ... helium atoms

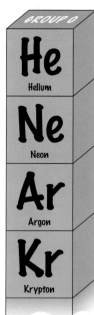

GROUP 0

He Helium
Ne Neon
Ar Argon
Kr Krypton

Uses Of The Noble Gases

- Helium is used in airships because it is much less dense than air.
- Argon is used in light bulbs because it is unreactive and provides an inert atmosphere.
- Argon, krypton and neon are all used in filament lamps and discharge tubes.

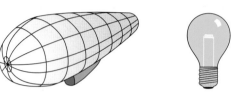

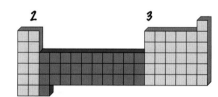

The Transition Metals

In the centre of the periodic table, between Groups 2 and 3, is a block of metallic elements called the TRANSITION METALS. These include: IRON, COPPER, PLATINUM, MERCURY, CHROMIUM and ZINC.

- These metals are HARD and MECHANICALLY STRONG (except mercury).
- They have HIGH MELTING POINTS (except mercury - which is liquid at room temperature).
- They are much LESS REACTIVE than Group 1 metals and do not react as quickly with oxygen or water.
- They form COLOURED COMPOUNDS which can be used as pottery glazes and can be seen in weathered copper which turns green.
- Many transition metals can be used as CATALYSTS in chemical reactions. Iron and platinum are used in this way to speed up certain chemical processes.
- In addition to these qualities, transition metals, like all other metals, are good conductors of heat and electricity, and can also be easily bent or hammered into shape.

These properties make transition metals very useful as structural materials, and as electrical and thermal conductors, for example ...

- ... in ELECTRICAL WIRING.
  - ... or PIPES ...
    ... in PLUMBING.

- Mixed with CARBON + ...
  ... small quantities of other metals ...
  in steel making.   • ... in CAST IRON SAUCEPANS.

COPPER

IRON

Trends Within Group 1

 LITHIUM ATOM 2,1

They all have ...

... SIMILAR PROPERTIES, because they have ...

... the SAME NUMBER OF ELECTRONS (ONE)

... in their OUTERMOST SHELL, ...

ie. the HIGHEST OCCUPIED ENERGY LEVEL ...

... CONTAINS ONE ELECTRON.

They become ...

... MORE REACTIVE ...

 SODIUM ATOM 2,8,1

... as we go down the group, because ...

... the OUTERMOST ELECTRON SHELL gets further away ...

... from the influence of the nucleus ...

... and so an electron is MORE EASILY LOST.

POTASSIUM ATOM 2,8,8,1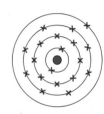

Trends Within Group 7

 FLUORINE ATOM 2,7

They all have ...

... SIMILAR PROPERTIES, because they have ...

... the SAME NUMBER OF ELECTRONS (SEVEN) ...

... in their OUTERMOST SHELL ...

ie. the HIGHEST OCCUPIED ENERGY LEVEL ...

... CONTAINS SEVEN ELECTRONS.

They become ...

... LESS REACTIVE ...

... as we go down the group, because ...

... the OUTERMOST ELECTRON SHELL gets further away ...

... from the influence of the nucleus ...

... and so an electron is LESS EASILY GAINED.

CHLORINE ATOM 2,8,7

Trends Within Group 0

 HELIUM ATOM 2

They all have ...

... SIMILAR PROPERTIES, because they have ...

... 'FULLY OCCUPIED' OUTERMOST SHELLS ...

ie. the HIGHEST OCCUPIED ENERGY LEVEL ...

... IS FULL.

NEON ATOM 2,8

Therefore ...

... they don't tend to GAIN ...

.. LOSE or SHARE ELECTRONS ...

... and therefore they are UNREACTIVE ...

... and MONATOMIC.

ARGON ATOM 2,8,8

Compounds of alkali metals and halogens have very different properties than the elements from which they are made. The use we make of these compounds depends on these different properties.

Industrial Electrolysis Of Sodium Chloride Solution (Brine)

Sodium chloride (common salt) is a compound of an **ALKALI METAL** and a **HALOGEN**.
It is found in large quantities in the sea and in underground deposits.
Electrolysis of sodium chloride solution produces ...

- **CHLORINE GAS** ...
  ... at the **POSITIVE ELECTRODE**.

- **HYDROGEN GAS** ...
  ... at the **NEGATIVE ELECTRODE**.

- **SODIUM HYDROXIDE SOLUTION** ...
  ... which is passed out of the cell.

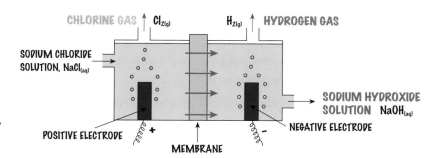

The products of the electrolysis of brine have many uses ...

<u>**CHLORINE ...**</u>

... is used to **KILL BACTERIA** in **DRINKING WATER** and **SWIMMING POOLS**.

... is used to manufacture **HYDROCHLORIC ACID, DISINFECTANTS, BLEACH** and the **PLASTIC, PVC**.

<u>**HYDROGEN ...**</u>

... is used in the manufacture of **AMMONIA** ...

... and **MARGARINE**.

<u>**SODIUM HYDROXIDE ...**</u>

... is used in the manufacture of **SOAP, ...**

... **PAPER, ...**

... and **CERAMICS**.

A simple laboratory test for chlorine ...
... is that it **BLEACHES DAMP LITMUS PAPER** ...
... ie. the chlorine removes the colour.

DAMP LITMUS PAPER BLEACHED BY CHLORINE.

Silver Halides

The main use of these halides is in the making of **PHOTOGRAPHIC FILM** and **PHOTOGRAPHIC PAPER**.
SILVER CHLORIDE, SILVER BROMIDE and **SILVER IODIDE** ...

... are **REDUCED** by **LIGHT** , **X-RAYS** 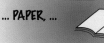 and **RADIATION** from **RADIOACTIVE SUBSTANCES** ...

... to **SILVER**, which is precipitated to form a photographic image.

Hydrogen Halides

These are all **GASES** which dissolve in water to produce **ACIDIC SOLUTIONS** ...
... eg. **HYDROGEN FLUORIDE (HF), HYDROGEN CHLORIDE (HCl)**
If we pass hydrogen chloride through water that contains universal indicator solution.

$HCl_{(g)}$ →

Beaker contains **WATER** and **UNIVERSAL INDICATOR** (green colour indicates water is neutral).

AFTER A FEW SECONDS

$HCl_{(g)}$ →

Beaker now contains **HYDROGEN CHLORIDE DISSOLVED IN WATER**, $HCl_{(aq)}$ (red colour indicates an acidic solution).

pH Scale

- When a substance dissolves in water it forms an AQUEOUS solution.
- The solution may be ACIDIC, ALKALINE or NEUTRAL.
- Water itself is neutral.

The pH scale is a measure of the acidity or alkalinity of an aqueous solution, across a 14 point scale.

VERY					SLIGHTLY	NEUTRAL	SLIGHTLY						VERY
1	2	3	4	5	6	7	8	9	10	11	12	13	14

- When substances dissolve in water, they dissociate into their individual IONS.
- Alkalis contain HYDROXIDE ions. $OH^-_{(aq)}$
- Acids contain HYDROGEN ions. $H^+_{(aq)}$

Indicators

These are really useful dyes which CHANGE COLOUR ...
 ... depending on whether they're in ACIDIC or ALKALINE solutions.
- Some are just simple substances such as LITMUS which changes from RED to BLUE or vice versa ...
- ... whereas others are mixtures of dyes, such as UNIVERSAL INDICATOR, which ...
- ... show a RANGE OF COLOUR to indicate just how ACIDIC or ALKALINE a substance is.

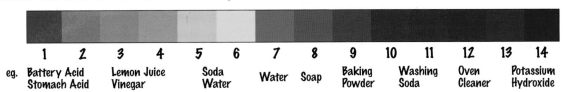

	1	2	3	4	5	6	7	8	9	10	11	12	13	14
eg.	Battery Acid Stomach Acid		Lemon Juice Vinegar		Soda Water		Water	Soap	Baking Powder		Washing Soda		Oven Cleaner	Potassium Hydroxide

Neutralisation

Because acids and alkalis are 'chemical opposites', if they are added together in the correct amounts they can 'cancel' each other out. This is called NEUTRALISATION because the solution which remains has a neutral pH of 7.

ACID + ALKALINE HYDROXIDE SOLUTION ⟶ NEUTRAL SALT SOLUTION + WATER

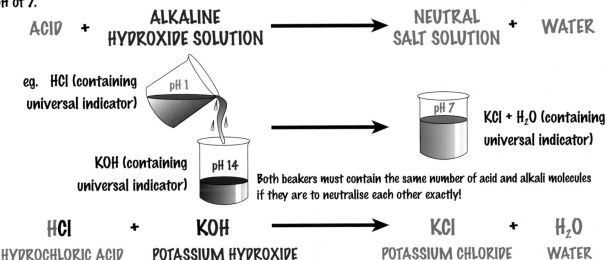

eg. HCl (containing universal indicator)
KOH (containing universal indicator)
KCl + H₂O (containing universal indicator)

Both beakers must contain the same number of acid and alkali molecules if they are to neutralise each other exactly!

HCl + KOH ⟶ KCl + H₂O
HYDROCHLORIC ACID   POTASSIUM HYDROXIDE   POTASSIUM CHLORIDE   WATER

HIGHER TIER

This can all be summarised more simply if we look at what's happening to the hydrogen ions $H^+_{(aq)}$ and the hydroxide ions $OH^-_{(aq)}$ in the acid and alkali:-

$$H^+_{(aq)} + OH^-_{(aq)} \longrightarrow H_2O_{(l)}$$

Salts Of Alkali Metals

Compounds of alkali metals, called SALTS, can be made by reacting solutions of their hydroxides (which are alkaline) with a particular acid. This is called a NEUTRALISATION REACTION and as we saw on the previous page, can be represented as follows:

ACID + ALKALINE HYDROXIDE SOLUTION ⟶ NEUTRAL SALT SOLUTION + WATER

The particular salt produced depends on the <u>METAL IN THE ALKALI</u>, and the <u>ACID USED</u>.

eg.   <u>SODIUM</u> HYDROXIDE + HYDRO<u>CHLORIC</u> ACID ⟶ <u>SODIUM CHLORIDE</u> + WATER

OTHER EXAMPLES

	HYDROCHLORIC ACID	SULPHURIC ACID	NITRIC ACID
+ SODIUM HYDROXIDE	⟶ SODIUM CHLORIDE + WATER	⟶ SODIUM SULPHATE + WATER	⟶ SODIUM NITRATE + WATER
+ POTASSIUM HYDROXIDE	⟶ POTASSIUM CHLORIDE + WATER	⟶ POTASSIUM SULPHATE + WATER	⟶ POTASSIUM NITRATE + WATER

Ammonia also dissolves in water to produce an alkaline solution. This can be neutralised with acids to produce ammonium salts.

+ AMMONIA	→ AMMONIUM CHLORIDE	→ AMMONIUM SULPHATE	→ AMMONIUM NITRATE

REMEMBER! THIS RULE ALWAYS APPLIES ...

- HYDROCHLORIC ACID produces <u>CHLORIDE</u> salts.
- SULPHURIC ACID produces <u>SULPHATE</u> salts.
- NITRIC ACID produces <u>NITRATE</u> salts.

Salts Of Transition Metals

Bases are the OXIDES and HYDROXIDES of metals. Those which are soluble are called ALKALIS. Unfortunately the OXIDES and HYDROXIDES of TRANSITION METALS are INSOLUBLE, which means that preparing their salts is a little less straightforward ...

- The metal OXIDE or HYDROXIDE is added to an acid until no more will react.
- The excess metal OXIDE or HYDROXIDE is then filtered off, ...
- ... to leave a solution of the salt which can then be evaporated to produce crystals of copper sulphate.

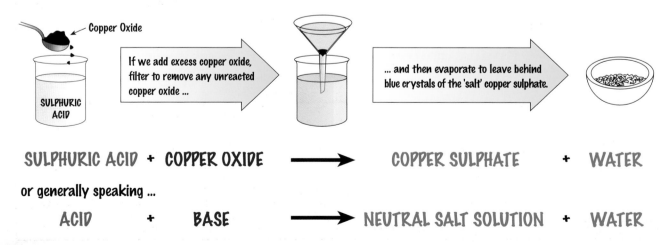

Copper Oxide

If we add excess copper oxide, filter to remove any unreacted copper oxide ...

SULPHURIC ACID

... and then evaporate to leave behind blue crystals of the 'salt' copper sulphate.

SULPHURIC ACID + COPPER OXIDE ⟶ COPPER SULPHATE + WATER

or generally speaking ...

ACID + BASE ⟶ NEUTRAL SALT SOLUTION + WATER

THE PERIODIC TABLE

- Elements in the same group have the same number of electrons in their outermost shell.
- Elements in the same group have similar properties.
- Going from left to right across a period the outer energy level is gradually filled with electrons.

EARLY ATTEMPTS TO CLASSIFY THE ELEMENTS

- John Newlands - arranged the known elements in order of relative atomic mass; he found similarities amongst every 8th element.
- Dimitri Mendeleev - left gaps to accommodate elements that had not been discovered.
- Modern Chemistry - discovery of electronic structure gives a more sound base for the table.

THE ELEMENTS OF GROUP 1

THE ALKALI METALS ...
- all have a LOW DENSITY
- have lower MELTING and BOILING POINTS as we go down the group.
- react with non-metals to produce IONIC COMPOUNDS ...

$$SODIUM + CHLORINE \longrightarrow SODIUM\ CHLORIDE$$
$$2Na_{(s)} + Cl_{2(g)} \longrightarrow 2NaCl_{(s)}$$

... which are WHITE SOLIDS and dissolve in water to form colourless solutions.
- react with water to produce HYDROXIDES and HYDROGEN

$$POTASSIUM + WATER \longrightarrow POTASSIUM\ HYDROXIDE + HYDROGEN$$
$$2K_{(s)} + 2H_2O_{(l)} \longrightarrow 2KOH_{(aq)} + H_{2(g)}$$

A simple laboratory test for the hydrogen gas produced ...
... is that when a test tube of hydrogen is held to a flame ...
... the hydrogen burns with a squeaky explosion (POP!)

TRENDS WITHIN GROUP 1
- Similar properties due to them having the same no. of electrons in their outermost shell.
- They become more reactive as we go down the group

THE ELEMENTS OF GROUP 7

THE HALOGENS ...
- all have LOW MELTING POINTS AND BOILING POINTS
- all have COLOURED VAPOURS • are BRITTLE and CRUMBLY when solid
- exist as MOLECULES • are POOR CONDUCTORS OF HEAT AND ELECTRICITY
- react with metals to produce IONIC SALTS.

LITHIUM + CHLORINE ⟶ LITHIUM CHLORIDE
- react with other non-metallic elements to form MOLECULAR COMPOUNDS.

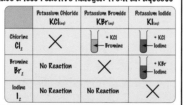

DISPLACEMENT REACTIONS OF THE HALOGENS
A more reactive halogen will displace a less reactive halogen from an aqueous solution of its salt.

	Potassium Chloride KCl(aq)	Potassium Bromide KBr(aq)	Potassium Iodide KI(aq)
Chlorine Cl₂	✕	+ KCl Bromine	+ KCl Iodine
Bromine Br₂	No Reaction	✕	+ KBr Iodine
Iodine I₂	No Reaction	No Reaction	✕

TRENDS WITHIN GROUP 7
- Similar properties due to them having the same no of electrons in outermost shell.
- They become less reactive as we go down group.

THE ELEMENTS OF GROUP 0 & TRANSITION METALS

THE NOBLE GASES ...
- all have LOW MELTING and BOILING POINTS
- are BRITTLE and CRUMBLY when SOLID
- are POOR CONDUCTORS of HEAT and ELECTRICITY
- exist as INDIVIDUAL ATOMS.

USES OF THE NOBLE GASES
- Helium is used in airships because it is much less dense than air.
- Argon is used in light bulbs because it is unreactive and provides an inert atmosphere.
- Argon, krypton and neon are all used in filament lamps and discharge tubes.

TRENDS WITHIN GROUP 0
- Similar properties as they have fully occupied outermost shells.
- They are unreactive and monatomic.

TRANSITION METALS
- Occupy central block of table
- EASILY BENT
- HIGH MELTING POINTS
- FORM COLOURED COMPOUNDS
- Include IRON, COPPER, ZINC and TIN
- GOOD CONDUCTORS OF HEAT & ELEC.
- HARD & TOUGH • Not too reactive
- Some are used as CATALYSTS.

COMPOUNDS OF ALKALI METALS AND HALOGENS

INDUSTRIAL ELECTROLYSIS OF SODIUM CHLORIDE SOLUTION
- CHLORINE GAS ...
  ... at the POSITIVE ELECTRODE.
- HYDROGEN GAS ...
  ... at the NEGATIVE ELECTRODE.
- SODIUM HYDROXIDE SOLUTION ...
  ... which is passed out of the cell.

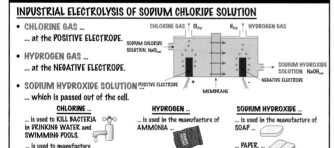

CHLORINE ...
... is used to KILL BACTERIA in DRINKING WATER and SWIMMING POOLS.
... is used to manufacture HYDROCHLORIC ACID, DISINFECTANTS, BLEACH and the PLASTIC PVC.

HYDROGEN ...
... is used in the manufacture of AMMONIA ...
... and MARGARINE.

SODIUM HYDROXIDE ...
... is used in the manufacture of SOAP ...
... PAPER ...
... and CERAMICS.

SILVER HALIDES
SILVER CHLORIDE, SILVER BROMIDE and SILVER IODIDE ...
... are REDUCED by LIGHT , X-RAYS and RADIATION from
RADIOACTIVE SUBSTANCES ...
... to SILVER, which is precipitated to form a photographic image.

HYDROGEN HALIDES
These are all GASES which dissolve in water to produce ACIDIC SOLUTIONS.

pH, INDICATORS, NEUTRALISATION + SALTS

Acids contain HYDROGEN H^+ ions. Alkalis contain HYDROXIDE OH^- ions.
Universal indicator is a mixture of dyes which changes colour at different pHs.

NEUTRALISATION ...
ACID + ALKALINE HYDROXIDE ⟶ NEUTRAL SALT + WATER
SOLUTION   SOLUTION

eg. Hydrochloric + Potassium ⟶ Potassium + Water
    Acid   Hydroxide   Chloride

$$H^+_{(aq)} + OH^-_{(aq)} \longrightarrow H_2O_{(l)}$$

PREPARING SALTS ...
the salt produced in a reaction between an acid and an alkali depends on ...
.. • THE ACID USED .. • THE METAL IN THE ALKALI
HYDROCHLORIC ACID + SODIUM HYDROXIDE ⟶ SODIUM CHLORIDE + WATER
In neutralisation reactions ...
  HYDROCHLORIC ACID produces CHLORIDE SALTS
  SULPHURIC ACID produces SULPHATE SALTS
  NITRIC ACID produces NITRATE SALTS

SALTS OF TRANSITION METALS ...
because their OXIDES and HYDROXIDES are INSOLUBLE they must be added to acid until no more will react, then filtered and evaporated to dryness.
SULPHURIC ACID + COPPER OXIDE ⟶ COPPER SULPHATE + WATER

1. The diagram below shows part of the periodic table.

								H									He
Li	Be											B	C	N	O	F	Ne
Na	Mg											Al	Si	P	S	Cl	Ar
K	Ca	Sc	Ti	V	Cr	Mn	Fe	Co	Ni	Cu	Zn	Ga	Ge	As	Se	Br	Kr

   a) What are the names of the elements represented by the following symbols:
   (i) Li (ii) N (iii) Ca (iv) Fe (v) K.
   b) Which element from the periodic table above has (i) the lowest atomic number? (ii) the highest atomic number? (iii) has an atomic number of 16? (Think about this before looking at a full periodic table!!)
   c) Give the names and symbols of THREE elements that are: (i) metals (ii) non-metals.

2. a) Why do elements in the same group have similar properties?
   b) Do elements in the same period have similar properties? Explain your answer.

3. Explain the work of John Newlands and Dimitri Mendeleev in their attempt to classify the elements.

4. Lithium, sodium and potassium are the first three elements in Group 1 of the periodic table.
   a) Explain why these elements form 1^+ IONS when they react with non-metals.
   b) A piece of sodium is added to water. A reaction takes place where a solution of sodium hydroxide and an unknown colourless gas are formed.
   (i) What is the name of this unknown gas?
   (ii) Describe a simple laboratory test for this gas.
   (iii) If universal indicator was present in the water explain, using diagrams, what would happen to the colour of the water when the sodium was added.
   c) A piece of potassium is added to water. Would you get a more vigorous or less vigorous reaction? Explain your answer.

5. Chlorine, bromine and iodine are three elements in Group 7 of the periodic table.
   a) Explain why these elements form 1^- IONS when they react with metals?
   b) The table below gives the melting and boiling points of chlorine, bromine and iodine in no particular order. Which element corresponds to 'X', 'Y' and 'Z'?

	X	Y	Z
MELTING POINT	114°C	-101°C	-7°C
BOILING POINT	184°C	-35°C	59°C

6. Complete the following displacement reactions. If there is no reaction write ' no reaction'.
   a) Potassium Chloride   +   Bromine ⟶
   b) Potassium Iodide   +   Bromine ⟶
   c) Potassium Bromide   +   Chlorine ⟶
   d) Potassium Bromide   +   Iodine ⟶

7. Helium, neon and argon are the first three elements in Group 0.
   a) What are these gases better known as?
   b) Write down the name of TWO other gases from this group.
   c) Explain why argon is a suitable gas for use in a filament lamp.

8. a) Name SIX transition metals.
   b) Which transition metal (i) has the symbol Hg? (ii) is used as a catalyst in the production of nitric acid?

9. Why is copper used for a) electrical wiring? b) pipes in plumbing?

10. Explain why:
    a) Elements in Group 1 have similar properties and their reactivity <u>increases</u> as we go down the group.
    b) Elements in Group 7 have similar properties and the reactivity <u>decreases</u> as we go down the group.
    c) Elements in Group 0 have similar properties and are unreactive.

11. Chlorine, hydrogen and sodium hydroxide are all made by the electrolysis of sodium chloride solution.
    The diagram below shows the electrolysis cell used.
    a) Name 'A', 'B' and 'C'.
    b) The products all have their particular uses.
    Which product is used in the manufacture of
    (i) margarine? (ii) disinfectants? (iii) fertilisers? (iv) soap?

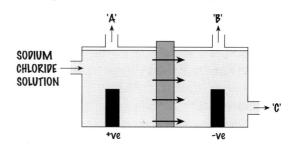

12. The beaker below (1) contains water with a few drops of universal indicator added to it.

 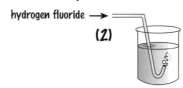

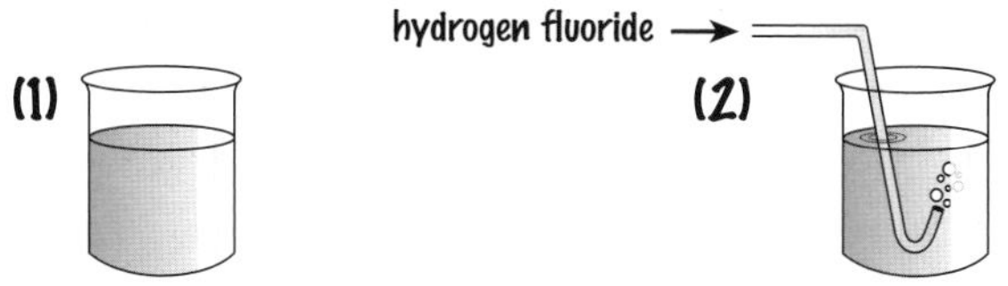

    a) What colour would the water become? Explain your answer.
    b) Some hydrogen fluoride gas is passed into the water as shown above (2).
    (i) What colour would the water become? (ii) Explain your answer.

13. a) What colour would (i) lemon juice (ii) washing soda and (iii) soda water turn in universal indicator?
    b) Copy and complete the following equation.

$$\text{Acid} \quad + \quad \text{Alkali} \quad \longrightarrow$$

14. Which ONE of the following would produce (i) a neutral (ii) an acidic and (iii) an alkali solution.
    All solutions are the same strength!
    A) $100cm^3$ of hydrochloric acid is added to $90cm^3$ of sodium hydroxide.
    B) $100cm^3$ of hydrochloric acid is added to $100cm^3$ of sodium hydroxide.
    C) $100cm^3$ of hydrochloric acid is added to $110cm^3$ of sodium hydroxide.
    Explain your answers.

15. Copy and complete the following word equations.
    a) Sulphuric Acid + Calcium Hydroxide ⟶
    b) Nitric Acid + Sodium Hydroxide ⟶
    c) Hydrochloric Acid + Potassium Hydroxide ⟶
    d) Sulphuric Acid + Ammonia ⟶

16. a) What is a base?
    b) Complete the following equation:
    Hydrochloric Acid + Copper Oxide ⟶
    c) How would you obtain crystals of the 'salt' formed?

Chemical reactions only occur when **REACTING PARTICLES COLLIDE WITH EACH OTHER** with sufficient energy to react. The minimum amount of energy required to cause this reaction is called the **ACTIVATION ENERGY**. There are **FOUR** important factors which affect the **RATE OF REACTION**:

TEMPERATURE, CONCENTRATION, SURFACE AREA and **USE OF A CATALYST**.

Temperature Of The Reactants

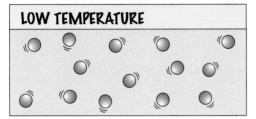

LOW TEMPERATURE

FASTER SPEED ... ... MORE COLLISIONS.

HIGH TEMPERATURE

In a COLD reaction mixture the particles are moving quite SLOWLY - the particles will collide with each other less often, with less energy, and less collisions will be successful.

If we HEAT the reaction mixture the particles will move more QUICKLY - the particles will collide with each other more often, with greater energy, and many more collisions will be successful.

Concentration Of The Dissolved Reactants

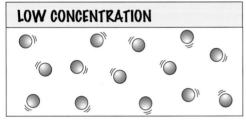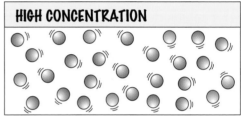

LOW CONCENTRATION

MORE PARTICLES ... ... MORE COLLISIONS.

HIGH CONCENTRATION

In a reaction where one or both reactants are in LOW concentrations the particles are spread out and will collide with each other less often resulting in fewer successful collisions.

In a reaction where one or both reactants are in HIGH concentrations the particles are crowded close together and will collide with each other more often, resulting in an increased number of successful collisions.

We see a similar effect when the reactants are GASES. As we increase the pressure on a gas, we push the particles closer together - they will then collide more often and the reaction will be faster.

LOW PRESSURE

RATE OF REACTION INCREASES

HIGH PRESSURE

Surface Area Of Solid Reactants

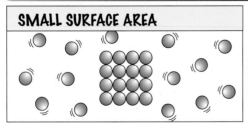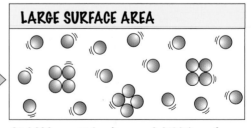

SMALL SURFACE AREA

BIGGER SURFACE AREA ... ... MORE COLLISIONS.

LARGE SURFACE AREA

LARGE particles have a SMALL surface area in RELATION TO THEIR VOLUME - less particles are exposed and available for collisions. This means less collisions and a slower reaction.

SMALL particles have a LARGE surface area in RELATION TO THEIR VOLUME - more particles are exposed and available for collisions. This means more collisions and a faster reaction.

REACTION RATE IS SLOW

... where

 = SURFACE AREA

REACTION RATE IS FASTER

Using A Catalyst

A CATALYST is a substance which INCREASES the RATE of a chemical reaction, without being used up in the process. It can be used over and over again to increase the rate of conversion of reactants into products.

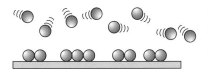

A catalyst lowers the amount of energy needed for a successful collision - so more collisions will be successful and the reaction will be faster. Also it provides a surface for the molecules to attach to, thereby increasing their chances of bumping into each other.

Catalysts are SPECIFIC ie. different reactions need different catalysts ...

eg. • the cracking of hydrocarbons uses BROKEN POTTERY.
   • the manufacture of ammonia (Haber process) uses IRON.

Increasing the rates of chemical reactions is important in industry because it helps to reduce costs.

Analysing The Rate Of Reaction

The rate of a chemical reaction can be analysed in TWO ways:

   1. Measure the rate at which reactants are used up.

   2. Measure the rate at which products are formed.

EXAMPLE ... the decomposition of hydrogen peroxide using manganese (IV) oxide.

HYDROGEN PEROXIDE ⟶ WATER + OXYGEN

Measure the mass of the reaction mixture.
Oxygen is produced and so the mass of the reaction mixture will <u>decrease</u>.

Measure the volume of <u>oxygen produced</u>.
A gas syringe can be used.

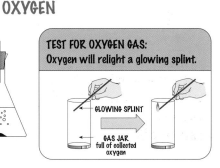

TEST FOR OXYGEN GAS:
Oxygen will relight a glowing splint.

GLOWING SPLINT

GAS JAR
full of collected
oxygen

GRAPHS can then be plotted to show the progress of a chemical reaction - there are THREE things to remember.

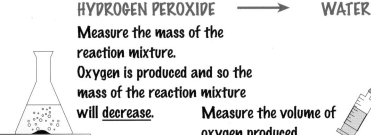

1 | When one of the reactants is used up the reaction stops (line becomes flat).

2 | The same amount of product is formed from the same amount of reactants, irrespective of rate.

3 | The steeper the line the faster the reaction.

REACTION A IS FASTER THAN REACTION B - this could be for one of four reasons:

The SURFACE AREA of the solid reactants in A is GREATER than in B.	The CONCENTRATION of the solution in A is GREATER than in B.
The TEMPERATURE of reaction A is GREATER than reaction B.	A CATALYST is used in reaction A but NOT in reaction B.

ENZYMES are biological catalysts. They are PROTEIN MOLECULES and they control the RATE OF REACTIONS which occur in living organisms. These reactions take place in cells in order to produce new materials.

Fermentation

Under the right temperature conditions enzymes in YEAST CELLS convert SUGAR into ALCOHOL (ethanol) and CARBON DIOXIDE which is given off in the reaction. This is FERMENTATION and it can easily be demonstrated ...

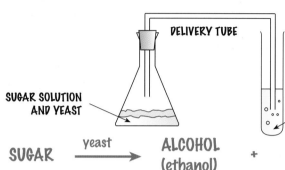

DELIVERY TUBE

SUGAR SOLUTION AND YEAST

A SIMPLE LABORATORY TEST FOR THE CARBON DIOXIDE GIVEN OFF IS THAT IT TURNS LIME-WATER MILKY.

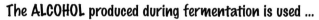

SUGAR →(yeast)→ ALCOHOL (ethanol) + CARBON DIOXIDE

The ALCOHOL produced during fermentation is used ...
... as the basis for the BREWING and WINE-MAKING INDUSTRIES.

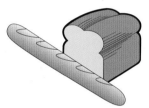

The bubbles of CARBON DIOXIDE produced is used in BAKING ...
... to make the bread rise.

Yoghurt Making

Enzymes in bacteria produce yoghurt from milk ...
... by converting lactose, ...
... a sugar found in milk, to LACTIC ACID ...
... so giving it a slightly sour taste.

Optimum Conditions For Enzymes

• The OPTIMUM CONDITIONS are the conditions under which enzymes work best ...
  ... this is usually AROUND 37°C for most enzymes ...
  ... below this temperature the rate of reaction is SLOW ... above 45°C the enzyme becomes DENATURED.
  Denaturing means that the enzyme is permanently destroyed.
• Different enzymes work better at different pHs. At extremes of pH enzymes become DENATURED.

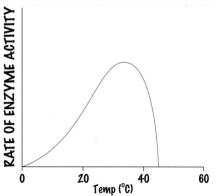

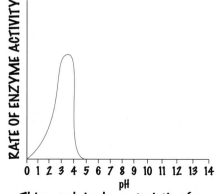

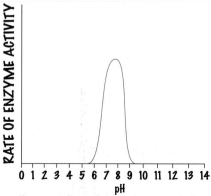

• This graph is characteristic of most body enzymes.

• This graph is characteristic of the enzyme, protease, produced by the stomach.

• This graph is characteristic of the enzymes released into and produced by the small intestine.

Enzymes have many uses, both domestically, and also in industrial processes where they are used to make reactions occur at normal temperatures and pressures that would otherwise require expensive, energy-demanding equipment.

Examples

1. BIOLOGICAL DETERGENTS

These contain enzymes such as PROTEASES and LIPASES which can digest and therefore remove tough stains from clothes ...
... at LOWER TEMPERATURES than would otherwise be needed.

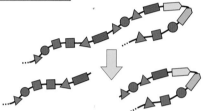

2. BABY FOODS

Proteases are sometimes used to 'pre-digest' the protein in some baby foods in order to make them easier to absorb by the infant. Long protein molecules are cleaved into shorter chains of amino acids.

3. CONVERSION OF STARCH TO SUGAR

Carbohydrases can be used to convert starch syrup to sugar syrup so that it can be used as a sweetener in various fillings etc. The sugars produced may be sucrose (as shown in the diagram) or glucose depending on the enzymes used.

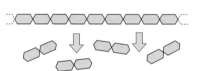

4. CONVERSION OF GLUCOSE INTO FRUCTOSE

Glucose and fructose are isomers. This means that they have the same chemical formula but their atoms are arranged in slightly different ways. Glucose can be changed to fructose by isomerase. Fructose is much sweeter and so less is required to sweeten foods. This makes it ideal in slimming foods.

HIGHER TIER

Batch v Continuous Production

- In batch production, the enzyme is mixed with the substrate and left to catalyse the reaction in large reactor vessels. At the end, the product has to be separated from the enzyme, which is expensive, or the enzyme written off and replaced by a new enzyme, which is also expensive.
- In continuous production, the enzyme is IMMOBILISED by attaching it to an inert solid such as resin beads or trapping it inside an alginate gel. This enables the substrate to be constantly poured through the enzyme-immobiliser complex allowing the product molecules to run out free of any enzymes. Obviously since there is no need for separation, this process is cheaper.

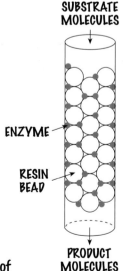

SUBSTRATE MOLECULES

ENZYME

RESIN BEAD

PRODUCT MOLECULES

Enzyme 'Shelf Life'

- Because enzymes are protein molecules they are fairly large molecules, consisting of a chain of individual amino acids. Consequently this means that they are fairly delicate and may be easily denatured.

- In order to prevent this, they are stabilised so that unusual pH's or temperatures don't affect them. This usually involves some kind of barrier which prolongs their natural shelf life.

Reversible Reactions

Some chemical reactions are REVERSIBLE - ie. the products can react to produce the original reactants.

$$A + B \rightleftharpoons C + D$$

A and B react to produce C and D, but also C and D can react to produce A and B.

$$\text{AMMONIUM CHLORIDE} \rightleftharpoons \text{AMMONIA} + \text{HYDROGEN CHLORIDE}$$

$$NH_4Cl_{(s)} \rightleftharpoons NH_{3(g)} + HCl_{(g)}$$

Solid AMMONIUM CHLORIDE ...
... decomposes when heated ...
... to produce AMMONIA ...
... and HYDROGEN CHLORIDE gas, ...
... both of which are colourless.

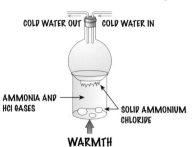

COLD WATER OUT   COLD WATER IN

AMMONIA AND
HCl GASES

SOLID AMMONIUM
CHLORIDE

WARMTH

AMMONIA reacts with ...
... HYDROGEN CHLORIDE gas ...
... to produce clouds of ...
... white AMMONIUM CHLORIDE powder.

HIGHER TIER

Reversible Reactions In Closed Systems

When a reversible reaction occurs in a CLOSED SYSTEM where NO REACTANTS are added and NO PRODUCTS are removed then an EQUILIBRIUM is achieved where the reactions occur at exactly the same rate in both directions. The relative amounts of all the reacting substances at equilibrium depends on the conditions of the reaction. If we take the reaction ...

$$A + B \rightleftharpoons C + D$$

$$\boxed{A} + \boxed{B} \rightleftharpoons \boxed{C} + \boxed{D}$$

- If the forward reaction (the reaction that produces the products C and D) is ENDOTHERMIC ...
  ... ie. a reaction that takes in energy (see next page) then ...

  IF THE TEMPERATURE IS INCREASED ... $\boxed{A} + \boxed{B} \rightleftharpoons \boxed{C} + \boxed{D}$ ... THE YIELD OF PRODUCTS IS INCREASED.

  IF THE TEMPERATURE IS DECREASED ... $\boxed{A} + \boxed{B} \rightleftharpoons \boxed{C} + \boxed{D}$ ... THE YIELD OF PRODUCTS IS DECREASED.

- If the forward reaction is EXOTHERMIC ie. a reaction that gives out energy (see next page) then ...

  IF THE TEMPERATURE IS INCREASED ... $\boxed{A} + \boxed{B} \rightleftharpoons \boxed{C} + \boxed{D}$ ... THE YIELD OF PRODUCTS IS DECREASED.

  IF THE TEMPERATURE IS DECREASED ... $\boxed{A} + \boxed{B} \rightleftharpoons \boxed{C} + \boxed{D}$ ... THE YIELD OF PRODUCTS IS INCREASED.

Gaseous Reactions

In gaseous reactions, an INCREASE IN PRESSURE favours the reaction which produces the least number of molecules ...

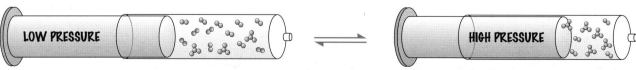

LOW PRESSURE $\rightleftharpoons$ HIGH PRESSURE

NB These factors above, along with reaction rates, determine the optimum conditions in industrial processes. An important example is the HABER PROCESS (see P.36 and 37).

Many chemical reactions are accompanied by a temperature change.

Exothermic Reactions

These reactions are accompanied by a TEMPERATURE RISE. They are known as EXOTHERMIC reactions because HEAT ENERGY is transferred TO THE SURROUNDINGS. Combustion is a common example of an exothermic reaction ...

METHANE + OXYGEN ⟶ CARBON DIOXIDE + WATER + HEAT ENERGY
(natural gas)

CARBON + OXYGEN ⟶ CARBON DIOXIDE + HEAT ENERGY
(coal)

OCTANE + OXYGEN ⟶ CARBON DIOXIDE + WATER + HEAT ENERGY
(in petrol)

- It is not only reactions between fuels and oxygen which are exothermic! For example neutralising alkalis with acids gives out heat too!

Endothermic Reactions

These reactions are accompanied by a FALL IN TEMPERATURE. They are known as ENDOTHERMIC reactions because HEAT ENERGY is transferred FROM THE SURROUNDINGS. Dissolving ammonium nitrate crystals in water is an endothermic reaction ...

AMMONIUM NITRATE + WATER ⟶ AMMONIUM NITRATE SOLUTION − HEAT ENERGY

$NH_4NO_{3(s)}$ + $H_2O_{(l)}$ ⟶ $NH_4NO_{3(aq)}$

The temperature has fallen by 7°C!

Reversible Reactions

If a reaction is REVERSIBLE and it is EXOTHERMIC IN ONE DIRECTION ...
... then it follows that it is ENDOTHERMIC IN THE OPPOSITE DIRECTION ...
... with the SAME AMOUNT of ENERGY being transferred in each case.
If we take hydrated copper sulphate and gently heat it ...

HYDRATED COPPER SULPHATE (blue) + HEAT ENERGY ⇌ ANHYDROUS COPPER SULPHATE (white) + WATER

$CuSO_4 . 5H_2O_{(s)}$ ⇌ $CuSO_{4(s)}$ + $5H_2O_{(l)}$

If WATER is added to white ANHYDROUS COPPER SULPHATE, blue HYDRATED COPPER SULPHATE is formed as heat is given out.

Blue crystals of HYDRATED COPPER SULPHATE become white ANHYDROUS COPPER SULPHATE on heating, as WATER is removed.

The reverse reaction above can be used as a test for water where the colour change from white to blue is an indication of the presence of water.

Making And Breaking Bonds

In a chemical reaction new substances are produced. In order to do this the BONDS in the reactants must be BROKEN, and new BONDS in the products must be MADE.

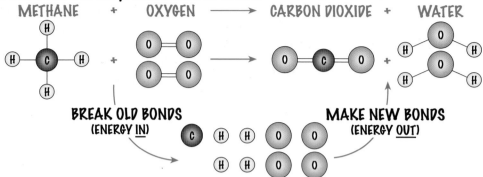

METHANE + OXYGEN → CARBON DIOXIDE + WATER

BREAK OLD BONDS (ENERGY IN)

MAKE NEW BONDS (ENERGY OUT)

- Breaking a chemical bond is hard work - a lot of energy has to be put IN.
- If energy is going IN this must be an ENDOTHERMIC process.
- When a new chemical bond is made - energy is given OUT.
- As energy is being given OUT, this must be an EXOTHERMIC process.
- BREAKING bonds is ENDOTHERMIC, MAKING bonds is EXOTHERMIC.

We can use this idea to find out if a chemical reaction is exo- or endothermic.

ENDOTHERMIC

If MORE energy is NEEDED to break old bonds than is released when new bonds are made, the reaction must be ENDOTHERMIC.

EXOTHERMIC

If MORE energy is RELEASED when new bonds are made than is needed to break the old bonds, the reaction must be EXOTHERMIC.

Energy Level Diagrams

The energy changes in a chemical reaction can be illustrated using an ENERGY LEVEL DIAGRAM.

① Exothermic Processes

In an exothermic reaction energy is given OUT. This means energy is being LOST so the products have less energy than the reactants.

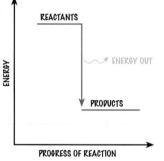

② Endothermic Processes

In an endothermic reaction, energy is being taken IN. This means that energy is being GAINED, so the products have more energy than the reactants.

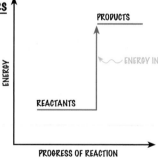

③ Activation Energy

The ACTIVATION ENERGY is the energy needed to start a reaction ie. to break the old bonds. We can show this on an energy level diagram too.

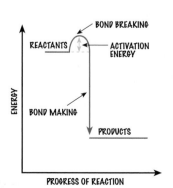

④ Catalysts

CATALYSTS reduce the activation energy for a reaction - this makes the reaction go faster.

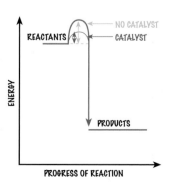

Examples Of Bond Energies

- We have seen that energy is NEEDED to BREAK bonds,
  ... and energy is RELEASED when MAKING bonds.

The AMOUNT of energy involved when bonds are broken or made depends on the particular bonds you are dealing with.

We can look up these BOND ENERGIES in data books (you will be told them in an exam question) and use them to find out how much energy is taken in or released in a reaction.

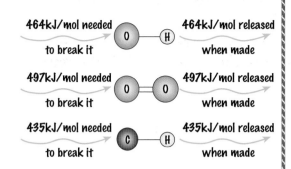

464kJ/mol needed to break it — O—H — 464kJ/mol released when made

497kJ/mol needed to break it — O=O — 497kJ/mol released when made

435kJ/mol needed to break it — C—H — 435kJ/mol released when made

- The units are kilojoules per mole.

Calculating Nett Energy Transfers Using Bond Energies

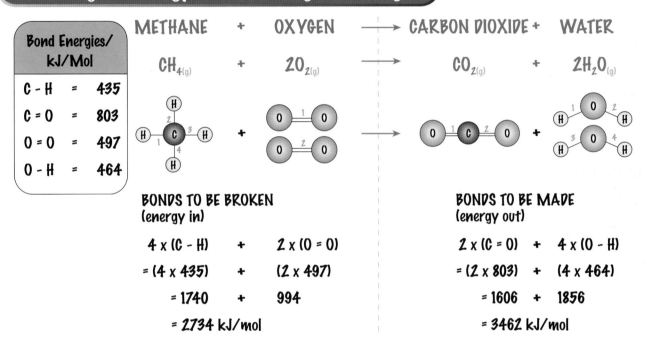

METHANE + OXYGEN → CARBON DIOXIDE + WATER

$CH_{4(g)}$ + $2O_{2(g)}$ → $CO_{2(g)}$ + $2H_2O_{(g)}$

Bond Energies/ kJ/Mol		
C - H	=	435
C = O	=	803
O = O	=	497
O - H	=	464

BONDS TO BE BROKEN
(energy in)

$4 \times (C - H)$ + $2 \times (O = O)$

$= (4 \times 435)$ + (2×497)

$= 1740$ + 994

$= 2734$ kJ/mol

BONDS TO BE MADE
(energy out)

$2 \times (C = O)$ + $4 \times (O - H)$

$= (2 \times 803)$ + (4×464)

$= 1606$ + 1856

$= 3462$ kJ/mol

So 2734 kJ/mol go IN and 3462 kJ/mol go OUT.

The difference is 2734 - 3462 = -728 kJ/mol of energy being given OUT (since it is negative).

This is an EXOTHERMIC REACTION.

Energy Level Diagrams

We can also use energy level diagrams to find the energy change for a chemical reaction.

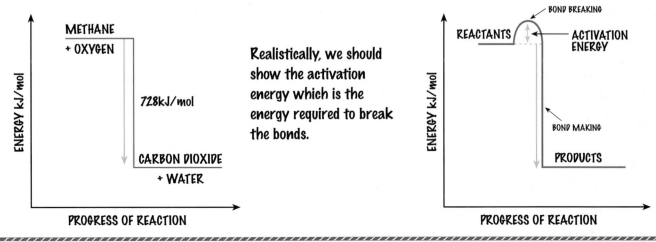

Realistically, we should show the activation energy which is the energy required to break the bonds.

RATES OF REACTION

TEMPERATURE
• Higher temperature results in increased rate of reaction.

'COOL' 'HOT' SLOW FAST

CONCENTRATION
• Greater concentration results in increased rate of reaction.

'DILUTE' 'CONCENTRATED' SLOW FAST

SURFACE AREA
• Greater area results in increased rate of reaction.
• Large particles = small surface area.
• Small particles = large surface area.

'BIG PIECES' 'TINY PIECES' SLOW FAST

CATALYSTS
• Lower the energy needed for a successful collision.
• Speed up a reaction without being used up.
These 4 factors affect the NUMBER OF SUCCESSFUL COLLISIONS
The rate of reaction can be followed by measuring the rate at which the products are formed or the reactants used up.

① When one of the reactants is used up the reaction stops (line becomes flat).
② The same amount of product is formed from the same amount of reactants, irrespective of rate.
③ The steeper the line the faster the reaction.

ENZYMES

Enzymes are biological catalysts. They are protein molecules that control the rate of reactions which occur in living organisms.

FERMENTATION
SUGAR —Yeast→ ALCOHOL + CARBON DIOXIDE
• Alcohol is used in the brewing and wine-making industries.
• Carbon dioxide is used in baking.

OPTIMUM CONDITIONS
These are the conditions under which enzymes work best. If the conditions vary from this optimum, then the enzymes are denatured.

USES OF ENZYMES
1. Biological detergents - contain proteases and lipases.
2. Baby foods - proteases are sometimes used.
3. Conversion of starch to sugar - carbohydrases used.
4. Conversion of glucose into fructose - isomerase used.

BATCH v CONTINUOUS PRODUCTION
• In batch production the enzyme has to be separated from the product at end of reaction or written off. An expensive process.
• In continuous production the enzyme is immobilised and there is no need for separation at end of reaction. A cheaper process.

REVERSIBLE REACTIONS

REVERSIBLE REACTIONS
A reversible reaction is one that can proceed in both directions.
A + B ⇌ C + D
A and B react to produce C and D, but also C and D can react to produce A and B.
AMMONIUM CHLORIDE ⇌ AMMONIA + HYDROGEN CHLORIDE

REVERSIBLE REACTIONS IN CLOSED SYSTEMS
When a reversible reaction occurs in a CLOSED SYSTEM where NO REACTANTS are added or NO PRODUCTS are removed then an EQUILIBRIUM is achieved where the reaction occurs at exactly the same rate in both directions.
• If the forward reaction is ENDOTHERMIC ...
IF THE TEMPERATURE IS INCREASED ... ... THE YIELD OF PRODUCTS IS INCREASED.
IF THE TEMPERATURE IS DECREASED ... ... THE YIELD OF PRODUCTS IS DECREASED.
• If the forward reaction is EXOTHERMIC ...
IF THE TEMPERATURE IS INCREASED ... ... THE YIELD OF PRODUCTS IS DECREASED.
IF THE TEMPERATURE IS DECREASED ... ... THE YIELD OF PRODUCTS IS INCREASED.

GASEOUS REACTIONS
In gaseous reactions, an INCREASE IN PRESSURE favours the reaction which produces the least number of molecules ...
LOW PRESSURE HIGH PRESSURE

EXOTHERMIC AND ENDOTHERMIC REACTIONS

EXOTHERMIC REACTIONS
These reactions are accompanied by a TEMPERATURE RISE. They are known as EXOTHERMIC reactions because HEAT ENERGY is transferred TO THE SURROUNDINGS. Combustion is a common example of an exothermic reaction ...
METHANE + OXYGEN → CARBON DIOXIDE + WATER + HEAT ENERGY (natural gas)
• It is not only reactions between fuels and oxygen which are exothermic! For example neutralising alkalis with acids gives out heat too!

ENDOTHERMIC REACTIONS
These reactions are accompanied by a FALL IN TEMPERATURE. They are known as ENDOTHERMIC reactions because HEAT ENERGY is transferred FROM THE SURROUNDINGS. Dissolving ammonium nitrate crystals in water is an endothermic reaction — AMMONIUM NITRATE + WATER → AMMONIUM NITRATE SOLUTION - HEAT ENERGY

REVERSIBLE REACTIONS
If a reaction is EXOTHERMIC IN ONE DIRECTION ... then it is ENDOTHERMIC IN THE OPPOSITE DIRECTION ...
HYDRATED COPPER SULPHATE (blue) + HEAT ENERGY ⇌ ANHYDROUS COPPER SULPHATE (white) + WATER
If WATER is added to white ANHYDROUS COPPER SULPHATE, blue HYDRATED COPPER SULPHATE is formed as heat is given out.
Blue crystals of HYDRATED COPPER SULPHATE becomes white ANHYDROUS COPPER SULPHATE on heating, as WATER is removed.
The reverse reaction above can be used as a test for water where the colour change from white to blue is an indication of the presence of water.

MAKING AND BREAKING BONDS

MAKING AND BREAKING BONDS
In a chemical reaction new substances are produced. In order to do this the BONDS in the reactants must be BROKEN, and new BONDS in the products must be MADE.

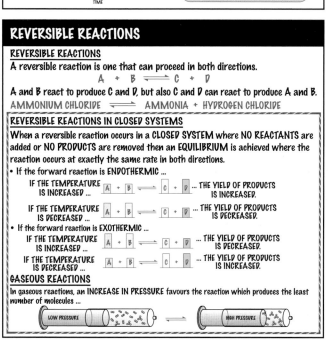

BREAK OLD BONDS (ENERGY IN) MAKE NEW BONDS (ENERGY OUT)

ENDOTHERMIC
If MORE energy is NEEDED to break old bonds, than is released when new bonds are made, the reaction must be ENDOTHERMIC.

EXOTHERMIC
If MORE energy is RELEASED when new bonds are made, than is needed to break the old bonds, the reaction must be EXOTHERMIC.

ENERGY LEVEL DIAGRAMS
Exothermic Processes | Endothermic Processes | Activation Energy | Catalysts

BOND ENERGIES

CALCULATING NETT ENERGY TRANSFERS USING BOND ENERGIES
eg. METHANE + OXYGEN → CARBON DIOXIDE + WATER
$CH_4(g)$ + $2O_2(g)$ → $CO_2(g)$ + $2H_2O(g)$

Bond Energies/ kJ/Mol	
C - H	435
C = O	803
O = O	497
O - H	464

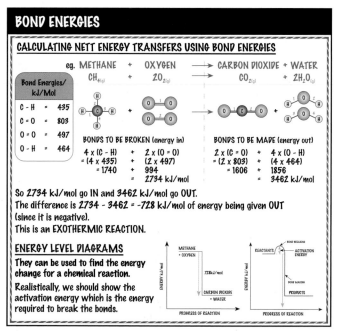

BONDS TO BE BROKEN (energy in)
4 x (C - H) + 2 x (O = O)
= (4 x 435) + (2 x 497)
= 1740 + 994
= 2734 kJ/mol

BONDS TO BE MADE (energy out)
2 x (C = O) + 4 x (O - H)
= (2 x 803) + (4 x 464)
= 1606 + 1856
= 3462 kJ/mol

So 2734 kJ/mol go IN and 3462 kJ/mol go OUT.
The difference is 2734 - 3462 = -728 kJ/mol of energy being given OUT (since it is negative).
This is an EXOTHERMIC REACTION.

ENERGY LEVEL DIAGRAMS
They can be used to find the energy change for a chemical reaction.
Realistically, we should show the activation energy which is the energy required to break the bonds.

1. Write down the FOUR factors which affect the rate of a chemical reaction.
   For each one explain how the reaction rate is affected.

2. What effect does pressure have on gaseous reactants? Explain your answer by means of a diagram.

3. a) Catalysts are specific. What does this mean?
   b) Give two examples.

4. a) Describe how you could monitor the rate of a chemical reaction against time.
   b) Below is a graph which shows the progress of three chemical reactions.

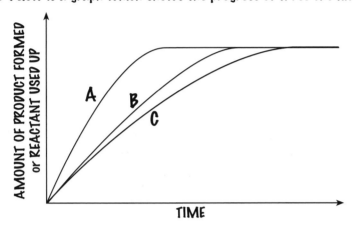

   i)   Which reaction was the fastest? Explain your answer.
   ii) Why does the line in the graph above become flat for all three reactions?
   iii) Give four possible reasons why the reactions progressed at different speeds.

5. a) What is an enzyme?
   b) The diagram below shows a simple experiment to show fermentation.

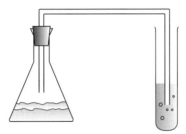

   i)   Write down a word equation for the reaction taking place.
   ii) Describe a simple laboratory test for this gas.
   iii) Explain how the products of fermentation are used in the food and drink industries.

6. The diagram below shows how the rate of a chemical reaction depends on the temperature.

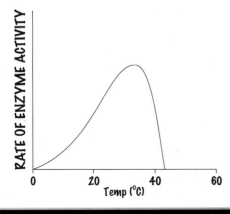

   a) What is meant by optimum temperature?
   b) How is the reaction affected if the temperature goes below the optimum temperature?
   c) How is the reaction affected if the temperature goes above the optimum temperature?

7. Explain how enzymes are used in biological detergents.

8. Which enzyme(s) is used ...
   a) to pre-digest baby food
   b) to convert starch into sugar
   c) to convert glucose into fructose

9. a) What is the difference between batch production and continuous production in enzyme-catalysed reactions?
   b) What is the advantage of immobilising an enzyme?

10. What is a reversible reaction?

11. a) A reversible reaction is carried out within a closed system. What does this mean?
    b) A reversible reaction is given by the equation.

$$A + B \rightleftharpoons C + D$$

If the forward reaction is endothermic which of the following shows the yield of reactants and products if the temperature is decreased. Explain your answer.

① 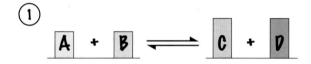   ②

12. Why does an increase in pressure favour the reaction which produces the least number of molecules in a gaseous reaction.

13. a) What are exothermic and endothermic reactions?
    b) Write TWO word equations for exothermic reactions.
    c) Write ONE word equation for an endothermic reaction.

14. a) Comment in as much detail as possible on the energy level diagram (i).

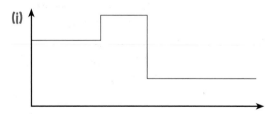   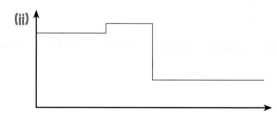

   b) Diagram (ii) is for the <u>same</u> reaction. Explain what could have caused the change.

15. Calculate the nett energy transfer when carbon reacts with oxygen to form carbon dioxide
    (Bond energies: O = O 497, C = O 803).

HAZARD SYMBOLS

Hazard	Symbol	Examples	Dealing with Spillage
Oxidising substances provide oxygen which allows other materials to burn more fiercely		Potassium Chlorate	Wear eye protection. Scoop the solid into a dry bucket. Rinse the area with water.
Highly Flammable substances easily catch fire.		Ethanol	Shut off all possible sources of heat or ignition. Open all windows to ventilate the area. Soak up the ethanol and dilute with water.
Toxic substances can cause death. They may have their effects when swallowed or breathed in or absorbed through the skin.		Chlorine	Evacuate the laboratory! Open a few outside windows to ventilate the room. Keep all internal doors closed.
Harmful substances are similar to toxic substances but less dangerous.		Iodine	Wear eye protection and gloves. Clear the iodine into a fume cupboard and add to sodium thiosulphate solution.
Corrosive substances attack and destroy living tissues, including eyes and skin.		1. Hydrochloric Acid 2. Sodium Hydroxide	1. Wear eye protection. Neutralise with sodium carbonate. Rinse area. 2. Wear eye protection. Neutralise with citric acid. Rinse area.
Irritants are not corrosive but can cause reddening or blistering of the skin.		Calcium Chloride	Wear eye protection. Scoop up solid and dissolve in water.

* Please note some spillages will be dealt with by laboratory technicians or teachers.

Key

Mass number →	1
	H
Atomic number (Proton number) →	1
	hydrogen

→ The lines of elements going across are called **periods**.

↓ The columns of elements going down are called **groups**.

Group 1	Group 2												Group 3	Group 4	Group 5	Group 6	Group 7	Group 8 or 0
																		4 **He** helium 2
7 **Li** lithium 3	9 **Be** beryllium 4												11 **B** boron 5	12 **C** carbon 6	14 **N** nitrogen 7	16 **O** oxygen 8	19 **F** fluorine 9	20 **Ne** neon 10
23 **Na** sodium 11	24 **Mg** magnesium 12												27 **Al** aluminium 13	28 **Si** silicon 14	31 **P** phosphorus 15	32 **S** sulphur 16	35 **Cl** chlorine 17	40 **Ar** argon 18
39 **K** potassium 19	40 **Ca** calcium 20	45 **Sc** scandium 21	48 **Ti** titanium 22	51 **V** vanadium 23	52 **Cr** chromium 24	55 **Mn** manganese 25	56 **Fe** iron 26	59 **Co** cobalt 27	59 **Ni** nickel 28	64 **Cu** copper 29	65 **Zn** zinc 30		70 **Ga** gallium 31	73 **Ge** germanium 32	75 **As** arsenic 33	79 **Se** selenium 34	80 **Br** bromine 35	84 **Kr** krypton 36
85 **Rb** rubidium 37	88 **Sr** strontium 38	89 **Y** yttrium 39	91 **Zr** zirconium 40	93 **Nb** niobium 41	96 **Mo** molybdenum 42	98 **Tc** technetium 43	101 **Ru** ruthenium 44	103 **Rh** rhodium 45	106 **Pd** palladium 46	108 **Ag** silver 47	112 **Cd** cadmium 48		115 **In** indium 49	119 **Sn** tin 50	122 **Sb** antimony 51	128 **Te** tellurium 52	127 **I** iodine 53	131 **Xe** xenon 54
133 **Cs** caesium 55	137 **Ba** barium 56	139 **La** lanthanum 57	178 **Hf** hafnium 72	181 **Ta** tantalum 73	184 **W** tungsten 74	186 **Re** rhenium 75	190 **Os** osmium 76	192 **Ir** iridium 77	195 **Pt** platinum 78	197 **Au** gold 79	201 **Hg** mercury 80		204 **Tl** thallium 81	207 **Pb** lead 82	209 **Bi** bismuth 83	210 **Po** polonium 84	210 **At** astatine 85	222 **Rn** radon 86
223 **Fr** francium 87	226 **Ra** radium 88	227 **Ac** actinium 89																

Lanthanides / Actinides:

140 **Ce** cerium 58	141 **Pr** praseodymium 59	144 **Nd** neodymium 60	147 **Pm** promethium 61	150 **Sm** samarium 62	152 **Eu** europium 63	157 **Gd** gadolinium 64	159 **Tb** terbium 65	162 **Dy** dysprosium 66	165 **Ho** holmium 67	167 **Er** erbium 68	169 **Tm** thulium 69	173 **Yb** ytterbium 70	175 **Lu** lutetium 71
232 **Th** thorium 90	231 **Pa** protactinium 91	238 **U** uranium 92	237 **Np** neptunium 93	242 **Pu** plutonium 94	243 **Am** americium 95	247 **Cm** curium 96	247 **Bk** berkelium 97	251 **Cf** californium 98	254 **Es** einsteinium 99	253 **Fm** fermium 100	256 **Md** mendelevium 101	254 **No** nobelium 102	257 **Lw** lawrencium 103

NOTES

THE COMPLETE KEY STAGE 3 PACKAGE ...

... 3 Course books

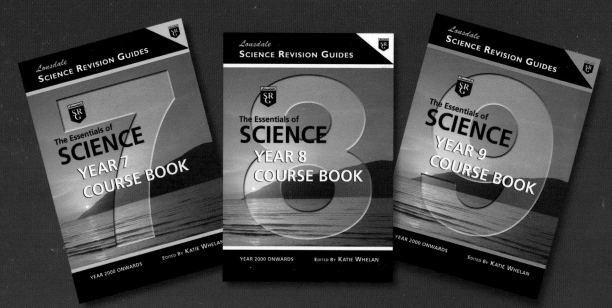

... matched perfectly to the QCA exemplar scheme of work for Key Stage 3.
All the content ... lots of exercises ... and an investigation for each unit.
These course books provide an inspection-proof scheme of work
for over-worked Science Departments.
Also there are 300 pages of differentiated internet support!

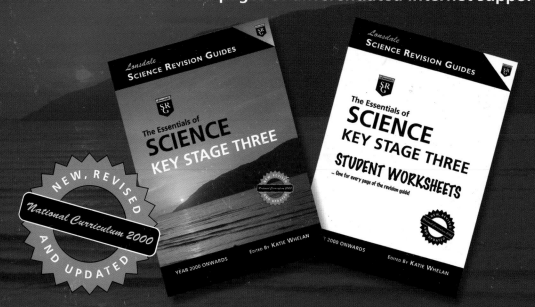

Plus ... the world famous **Revision Guide** and **Student Worksheets**.
These pull together all the information pupils need from years 7, 8 and 9 for
their Key Stage 3 National Curriculum Tests. They are completely revised and
updated for the new National Curriculum and contain everything the pupil
needs to revise ... and nothing more.